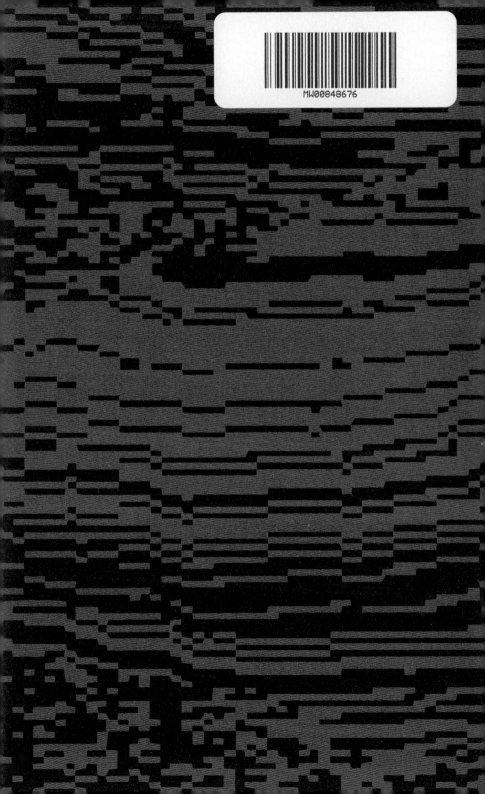

The Knitwear Manual

A COMPLETE GUIDE TO KNITWEAR DESIGN

FASHIONARY

ISBN 978-988-77111-8-6
SN KMV102408PBAT

Designed and published in Hong Kong
by Fashionary International Ltd
Printed in China

The Knitwear Manual is an ongoing project. If you have
any feedback, please don't hesitate to send it to
feedback@fashionary.org

 @ fashionary
 @ fashionary
 @ fashionary

Fashionary Team 2024

CONTENT

PREFACE

Knitwear holds a pivotal place in the fabric of fashion, seamlessly blending tradition with innovation. As a distinctive category, it demands specialized technical knowledge and a mastery of unique techniques in both design and production. The creation of knitwear is not just an art; it's a science that requires an intimate understanding of materials and a strong grasp of industrial production principles. For designers, the ability to navigate these complex waters is essential for both excellence in their craft and effective communication within the industry.

This book is meticulously crafted to serve as the quintessential guide in the realm of knits. This book delves deep into the intricacies of knitting, covering an extensive range of topics from the very fibers and yarns that form the foundation, through to the structures and styles that shape the final garment. Presented through a visually driven approach, the information is curated to be easily digestible, ensuring that designers find clarity amidst the technicalities.

It is with great enthusiasm that we present The Knitwear Manual to the design community. Our hope is that this book will not only become an invaluable tool in your design repertoire but also spark inspiration, pushing the boundaries of what can be achieved in knitwear.

FLOW CHART OF KNITWEAR MANUFACTURING

- - - → Optional
———→ Essential

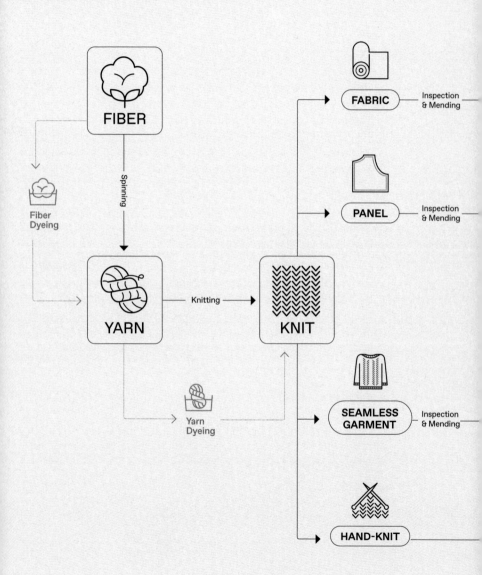

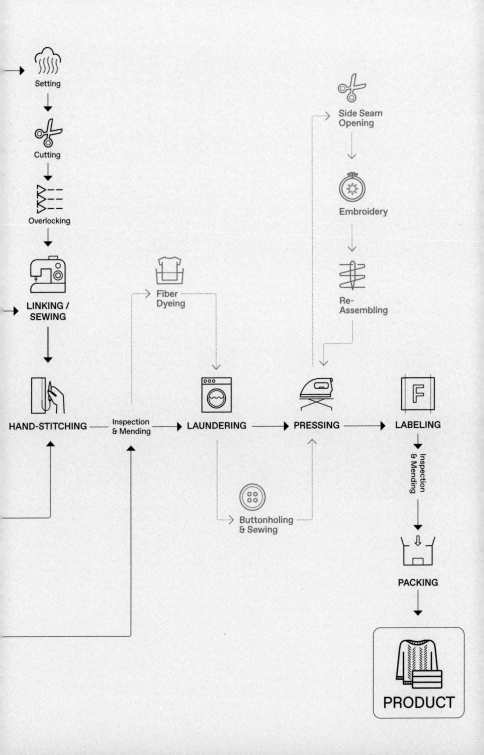

Setting

Cutting

Overlocking

LINKING / SEWING

HAND-STITCHING

Inspection & Mending

Fiber Dyeing

LAUNDERING

Buttonholing & Sewing

Side Seam Opening

Embroidery

Re-Assembling

PRESSING

LABELING

Inspection & Mending

PACKING

PRODUCT

CHAPTER 1

FIBER

The building block of knitting, fibers, dictate the texture, appearance, and functionality of the final piece. From animal to plant, synthetic to natural, understanding fibers' properties is critical to mastering the art and science of knitting.

1.1

FIBER CLASSIFICATION

Fibers, the raw materials for textile and apparel production, fall into two broad categories: natural fibers and man-made fibers, both integral to modern knitwear.

1.1.1
NATURAL FIBERS

ANIMAL FIBERS

These are protein-based complex substances derived from the coat of an animal, and are commonly used in knitting.

COMMON EXAMPLES

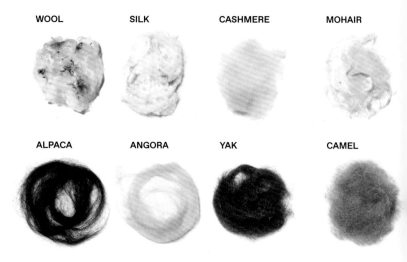

| WOOL | SILK | CASHMERE | MOHAIR |
| ALPACA | ANGORA | YAK | CAMEL |

PLANT FIBERS

These cellulose-based fibers are obtained from various parts of plants, including bast, seeds and shells.

COMMON EXAMPLES

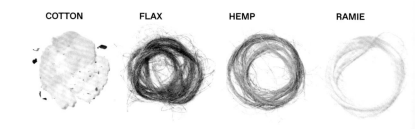

| COTTON | FLAX | HEMP | RAMIE |

1.1.2
MAN-MADE FIBERS

SYNTHETIC FIBERS
Synthetic fibers are made through chemical synthesis, and can be made into other fibers or fibrous forms.

FIBER SOURCE
Oil or coal

COMMON EXAMPLES

ACRYLIC

NYLON

POLYESTER

POLYURETHANE

REGENERATED FIBERS
Regenerated fibers are derived from natural resources, and go through a chemical transformation process.

FIBER SOURCE
Cellulose, wood pulp or protein.

COMMON EXAMPLES

RAYON

ACETATE

WOOL _WO_

Wool has a scaly, crimped structure that gives it excellent insulation and moisture-wicking properties. It has been used for thousands of years to produce high-quality yarn and knitting fabric.

COMMON VARIATIONS

The breed of a sheep plays a significant role in the fiber's quality. There are three common types of sheep's wool.

MERINO
Type of sheep:
Merino
Quality: Fine

SHETLAND
Type of sheep:
Crossbred sheep
Quality: Medium

LAMBSWOOL
Type of sheep:
6-to 7-month-old sheep
Quality: Fine

COMMON TYPES OF WOOL

WOOLEN	WORSTED
✎ Short fibers, 25.4-76.2mm	✎ Long fibers, longer than 76.2mm
⊘ Medium or coarse	⊘ Fine diameter
FABRIC APPEARANCE	FABRIC APPEARANCE
Soft and fuzzy	Crisp and smooth
CHARACTERISTICS	CHARACTERISTICS
▪ Insulator due to trapped air	▪ Less insulating
▪ Does not hold a crease well	▪ Holds creases and shape
▪ Less durable than worsted	▪ More durable than woolens

SURFACE

The scale pattern gives wool its moisture-absorbing properties. The scales can trap air, making wool a good insulator. The spiral shape of the scales also allows wool to stretch without breaking.

CHARACTERISTICS

- Weaker than flax
- Strength decreases when wet
- Holds garment shapes well
- Retains air and warmth
- High elasticity; considered the most extensible natural fiber
- Fades and weakens under continuous sunlight
- Mildew develops when wool is damp
- Possible irritant to skin
- Tends to shrink when wet
- Scales make it possible to be felted
- Wrinkle resistant
- Biodegradable
- Suitable for mechanical recycling with relativity long fibers

CARE

Hand wash cold with mild detergent or dry clean

Do not wring or twist

Do not tumble dry; dry flat is recommended

Steam or iron on a low to medium heat setting with a damp cloth

SILK *SE*

Silk is a luxurious natural fiber produced by silkworms. It is renowned for its softness, shine, and strength. Most silk fibers are continuous filaments composed of proteins secreted by silkworms in the formation of their cocoons.

TYPE OF SILK

The mulberry silkworm is the only cultivated silkworm. It also produces the best-quality silk.

MULBERRY	TUSSAH	ERI	MUGA
CN	IN/CN/JP	TH/IN	IN
*****	***	*	****
White	Deep gold	Off white	Honey gold
Filament	Filament	Spun	Filament

CARE

Hand wash cold with mild detergent or dry clean

Dry flat is recommended

Avoid direct sunlight when drying

Steam on low heat setting, inside out

SURFACE

The triangular, prism-like structure of silk fibers refracts light at different angles, which gives silk a shimmering appearance.

CHARACTERISTICS

- Smooth; drapes with a graceful flow
- One of the strongest natural fibers – stronger than cotton and linen
- Difficult to spin due to static electricity
- Poor conductor of heat
- Medium elasticity
- Absorbs and releases moisture quickly
- Sheds dust and dirt easily
- Takes dyes very well
- Tends to shrink
- Hypoallergenic
- Wrinkle resistant

CASHMERE *WS*

The undercoat of a cashmere goat's fleece. It has a similar structure to wool, but is softer and more luxurious.

MOHAIR *WM*

Mohair is a luxurious fiber derived from the Angora goat. It is known for its soft, silky texture, natural luster and elasticity.

SURFACE

Cashmere fibers are fine and smooth, with tiny scales that provide a soft, velvety texture. Its tightly packed scales bestow cashmere with its characteristic silky surface, loftiness, and warmth.

SURFACE

Mohair has smooth, flat scales that reflect light and give it a shiny appearance. Its semi-hollow structure makes it a good insulator.

CHARACTERISTICS

- Silky and extremely fine
- Soft; drapes with a graceful flow
- Retains warmth and is comfortable to wear
- Similar durability to wool and mohair
- Delicate and prone to pilling and abrasion
- Absorbs and retains moisture like wool
- Flame resistant
- Hypoallergenic
- Takes dye well

CHARACTERISTICS

- Natural sheen due to the reflection of large outer fiber scales
- High elasticity
- Absorbs and releases moisture
- Flame resistant
- Sheds dust and dirt more easily than wool
- Does not fade easily
- Takes dye exceptionally well
- Felts and shrinks less than wool
- Wrinkle resistant
- Biodegradable

CARE

Dry clean or hand wash in cool water

Do not wring or twist

Do not tumble dry; dry flat is recommended

Steam on low heat setting

CARE

Dry clean or hand wash in cool water

Do not wring or twist

Do not tumble dry; dry flat is recommended

Spruce up by lightly shaking or brushing the fabric

ALPACA *WP*

Alpaca is a lightweight and durable fiber from domesticated camelid animals. It has similar structure to wool, but is 1/3 lighter.

ANGORA *WA*

Angora fiber comes from the Angora rabbit and is known for its softness, warmth and silky texture. Its unique fuzzy texture closely resembles that of fur.

SURFACE

Alpaca fibers have a smoother surface with fewer scales than wool, resulting in a silkier, less itchy touch. The semi-hollow core of the fiber contributes to its lightness and thermal efficiency.

SURFACE

Angora fibers have a very thin, smooth surface with minimal scales. The fiber is exceptionally soft and the long fibers give angora its characteristic fluffiness.

CHARACTERISTICS

- Lightweight and very airy
- Very smooth and soft
- Felts readily, like wool
- More durable than wool
- Retains warmth, and is 3 to 5 times warmer than wool
- Breathable
- Flame resistant
- Hypoallergenic; does not irritate skin
- Limited color range due to difficulty bleaching
- Wrinkle and pill resistant
- Slightly gathers static electricity

CHARACTERISTICS

- Lightweight, soft and silky
- Very fine and fluffy, with a halo effect
- Retains warmth; can retain eight times more heat than wool
- Very low elasticity
- Absorbs and releases moisture quickly
- Easy to dye
- Felts easily through abrasion
- Anti-static

CARE

Dry clean or hand wash in cool water	Do not wring or twist	Do not tumble dry; dry flat is recommended	Steam on low heat setting

CARE

Dry clean or hand wash in cool water	Do not wring or twist	Do not tumble dry; dry flat is recommended	Avoid direct sunlight when drying

YAK *WY*

This luxurious fiber is made from the undercoat of yak. The fine yak fibers are considered warmer than merino, soft as cashmere, and tough as camel hair.

SURFACE

Yak fibers, similar to those of cashmere, feature small scales and a fine texture. The fibers are slightly more rigid, contributing to their resilience and warmth.

CHARACTERISTICS

- Soft but durable
- Shiny, and more lustrous than wool
- Wonderful drape, with good elasticity
- Difficult to spin
- Retains warmth, and is 10-15% warmer than wool
- More breathable than cashmere
- A sustainable alternative, as yak has less environmental impact than wool and cashmere

CARE

Hand wash cold with mild detergent or dry clean

Do not wring or twist

Do not tumble dry; dry flat is recommended

Steam on low heat setting

CAMEL HAIR *WK*

Camel hair is an excellent and luxurious thermoregulated fiber. It comes from the undercoat of two-humped (Bactrian) camels.

SURFACE

Camel hair has slightly irregular surface and sparse scale distribution, which provides a material that is robust yet soft to the touch. It also possesses a unique golden-tan shade that is difficult to bleach.

CHARACTERISTICS

- Lightweight, smooth and soft
- Lustrous
- Excellent insulating properties
- Lower elasticity than wool
- More sensitive to chemicals than wool
- Limited color range due to difficulty bleaching
- Does not tend to felt

CARE

Hand wash cold with mild detergent or dry clean

Do not wring or twist

Do not tumble dry; dry flat is recommended

Steam on low heat setting

COTTON *co*

Cotton is the most popular fiber in the world. It is highly absorbent and breathable, and can be worn year round. The fiber requires extensive processing to be made into fabric, and is widely used for knitwear.

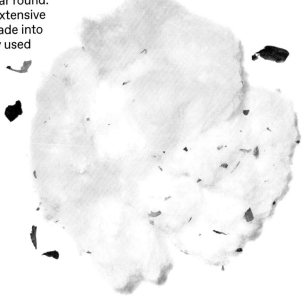

CLASSES OF COTTON

The grade of cotton depends on its cleanliness, whiteness, fiber length and strength.
A longer staple usually indicates higher quality, with a smoother hand feel.

STAPLE	LENGTH	CHARACTERISTICS
Extra Long	>35mm	Thin, long, smooth, soft and glossy
Long	30-65mm	Smooth and soft
Medium	20-30mm	More abundant
Short	<20mm	Thick, short, coarse

CARE

Machine wash in cool or warm water	Dry flat is recommended	Steam or iron on medium to high heat setting

SURFACE

Cotton fiber appears as a twisted, ribbon-like structure. It is made up of layers of cellulose molecules arranged in a spiral pattern.

CHARACTERISTICS

- Lightweight
- Durable; remains strong when wet
- Breathable and wearable all year round
- Absorbs and releases moisture very quickly
- Does not irritate skin
- Takes dye well but is prone to discoloration after washing
- Relatively stable but tends to shrink
- Prone to wrinkling
- Does not gather static electricity

FLAX *LI*

Flax is a very strong and durable raw material for producing linen. It is highly absorbent, breathable, and cool to the touch.

HEMP *CANHA*

A bast fiber from the Cannabis sativa plant, it has been used for centuries in textile production, prized for its durability and environmental sustainability.

SURFACE

Flax has cylindrical filaments with pointed edges. The filaments show irregular nodes or joints, resulting in a slightly uneven texture.

CHARACTERISTICS

- Slightly silky and lustrous
- Durable, stiff and crisp
- Can withstand high temperatures
- Breathable and cool to wear in summer
- Low elasticity
- Pill and insect resistant
- Absorbs and releases moisture very quickly
- Fades under continuous sunlight
- Takes dye well
- Fiber weakened by sodium hypochlorite bleach
- Softens after wash and wear
- Prone to wrinkling
- Anti-static
- Biodegradable

SURFACE

Hemp fibers have a long, irregular structure with a rough texture and visible nodes. It is a tough, durable fiber, and its irregular surface and inherent porosity enhance its absorbency.

CHARACTERISTICS

- 8 times stronger than cotton
- Highly durable
- Breathable and cool to wear in summer
- UV resistant
- Mildew and insect resistant
- Prone to wrinkling
- Hypoallergenic, does not irritate skin but can be scratchy due to coarse fiber
- Hard to dye with high lignin content
- Softens after wash and wear
- Not pliable and elastic, cannot be made into fine fabric
- A sustainable option as it is a low-maintainence plant that grows fast

CARE

Machine wash in cool or warm water

Do not bleach

Tumble dry low or dry flat

Steam or iron on high heat settings when damp

CARE

Hand wash or machine wash warm or cool

Do not bleach

Dry flat is recommended

Steam or iron on medium to high heat setting when damp

RAMIE *RA*

Ramie is highly absorbent and breathable, and is known for its strength and durability. The fiber has a silky luster and is often compared to linen.

ACETATE *AC*

Acetate is a man-made fiber derived from cellulose, typically created via acetic acid treatment. Sharing many properties with viscose rayon, it stands out for its distinctive high shine and excellent drape.

SURFACE

The ramie plant stalk contains a lot of gums and pectins, so it requires degumming to remove these substances and produce usable fiber.

SURFACE

The fibers have an attractive natural luster that can be controlled to achieve a shiny, semi-matte or matte appearance.

CHARACTERISTICS

- Stiff and brittle, but softens with age and washing
- Strength increases when wet
- Holds garment shapes well
- Increases in silkiness after washing
- Withstands high temperatures
- Low elasticity
- Releases moisture quickly
- More absorbent than cotton
- Antibacterial and mold resistant
- Takes dye well
- Doesn't shrink or lose its shape with repeated washing
- Prone to wrinkling and breakage when sharply creased
- Gathers static electricity

CHARACTERISTICS

- Smooth and soft
- Drapes with a graceful flow
- Highly breakable, especially when wet
- Low elasticity
- Pill resistant
- Does not absorb moisture well; dries fast
- Mildew and mold resistant
- Requires special dyes to be colorfast
- Prone to wrinkling
- Suitable for pleating due to its thermoplastic nature
- Gathers static electricity

CARE

Machine wash in cool or warm water | Do not bleach | Tumble dry low or dry flat | Steam or iron on high heat settings when damp

CARE

Machine wash in cool water | Tumble dry low or dry flat | Iron on low heat setting using a damp cloth

RAYON

Rayon, often referred to as artificial silk, is a versatile man-made cellulose fiber. It can be made into broad spectrum of yarn sizes and blends well with other fibers, lending a soft and silky touch to the fabric.

CHARACTERISTICS

- Smooth and soft
- Silky and lustrous
- Highly breakable, especially when wet
- Very absorbent but does not dry quickly
- Highly flammable
- Takes dye well
- Tends to shrink
- Good conductor of heat, suitable for summer wear

CARE

| Machine wash in cool or warm water | Do not bleach | Dry flat is recommended | Iron on low or medium setting |

VISCOSE *VI*

The terms "viscose rayon" and "viscose" are used interchangeably in the textile industry. It is a specific type of rayon made of wood pulp or other cellulosic material through viscose manufacturing process.

LYOCELL *LY/CLY*

A type of wood pulp fiber that is produced using an environmentally friendly, closed-loop chemical process. It has high tensile strength, good moisture absorption capability, and a soft feel to the touch.

CUPRO *CU*

Made from cellulosic pulp produced by cuprammonium process, cupro is renowned for its fluid drape. It possesses anti-static properties and is less prone to pilling.

MODAL *MD*

Crafted from beechwood pulp, it offers a smooth surface, softer hand and excellent drape, making it an ideal material for creating lingerie, bedding, and women's apparel.

ACRYLIC *PC*

Acrylic is a synthetic fiber made from a polymer called acrylonitrile. It is lightweight, soft and warm, and is often used as a wool substitute in knitted garments.

NYLON *PA*

Nylon was the first synthetic fiber; it was manufactured in the US in 1939. It is a thermoplastic material made from petrochemicals. Nylon 6 and Nylon 66 are the most commonly used types.

SURFACE
Wet-spun fibers have a kidney-shaped cross-section, while the dry-spun fibers have dog-bone-shaped cross-section. Acrylic closely resembles the look and feel of wool.

CHARACTERISTICS
- Lightweight and soft
- Wear-and-tear resistant
- Retains warmth
- Prone to pilling, often requires anti-pilling chemical treatment
- Moisture wicking and fast drying
- Highly UV resistant
- Chemical resistant; stable with common bleaching agents
- Mildew and insect resistant
- Takes dye and is colorfast
- Excellent dimensional stability
- Gathers static electricity

SURFACE
A cross-section of a nylon fiber can be changed easily, as the fibers are melt spun. A circular cross-section is the most common.

CHARACTERISTICS
- Smooth and soft
- Extremely durable, even when wet
- Heat sensitive and prone to melting
- High elasticity and excellent shape retention
- Wrinkle resistant
- Moisture wicking and fast drying
- Mildew and fungi resistant
- Takes dye well, but dark shades can fade during washing
- Easily gathers static electricity

CARE

Machine wash in cool or warm water | Fabric softener recommend | Tumble dry low or dry flat | Iron with low heat with pressing cloth

CARE

Hand wash or machine wash warm or cool | Do not use fabric softener | Tumble dry low or dry flat | Iron on low heat setting

POLYESTER *PL*

Polyester is a synthetic fiber made from petroleum-based materials. It is known for its durability, ease of care, and resistance to wrinkles and shrinking.

POLYURETHANE *PU*

A rubber-like material that can be used to make stretchable and durable knitwear.

The preferred name
SPANDEX (North America)
ELASTANE (Europe)
LYCRA® (UK/Spain/Australia)

SURFACE

Generally, polyester fibers are smooth and straight, and a cross-section is round. The fiber can be manufactured in different shapes and sizes for specific purposes.

CHARACTERISTICS

- Soft; drapes easily
- Holds garment shapes well
- Highly durable
- Retains pleats set by heat
- Pill resistant in filament form
- Fast drying
- Mildew and soil resistant
- Lower price point than most fabrics
- Takes dye well; requires high-temperature dye

SURFACE

The manufacturing process creates filaments that are circular in cross-section, but they can become non-circular while drying, due to the effects of solvent evaporation.

CHARACTERISTICS

- Lightweight, smooth and soft
- Highly durable
- Superior elasticity and recovery
- Pill resistant
- Oil and perspiration resistant
- Mildew and insect resistant
- Takes dye well
- Wrinkle resistant
- Abrasion resistant
- Anti-static

CARE

Machine wash in cool water | Do not use fabric softener | Tumble dry low or dry flat | Iron on low heat setting

CARE

Machine wash in cool or warm water | Do not use fabric softener | Tumble dry low or dry flat | Avoid high temperatures

1.2 FIBER COMPARISON

FIBER	TENSILE STRENGTH	MOISTURE ABSORPTION	ABRASION RESISTANCE	ELASTICITY	SHRINKAGE
WOOL	★	★★★	★	★★	★★★
SILK	★★	★★	★★	★★	★★
COTTON	★★	★★	★★	★	★★
FLAX	★★★	★★	★★	★	★★
ACETATE	★	★★	★	★★	★
RAYON	★	★★★	★★	★	★★
ACRYLIC	★★	★	★★	★★★	★★
NYLON	★★★	★	★★★	★★★	★
POLYESTER	★★★	★	★★★	★★★	★

	STATIC ELECTRICITY	PILLING	UV RESISTANCE	MOLD RESISTANCE	DRAPABILITY
WOOL	★★	★★★	★★	★★	★★
SILK	★★	★	★★	★★	★★
COTTON	★	★★	★	★	★★★
FLAX	★	★	★	★★	★★★
ACETATE	★★	★★	★	★★★	★★
RAYON	★★	★★	★	★★	★★★
ACRYLIC	★★★	★★★	★★★	★★★	★★
NYLON	★★★	★★★	★★★	★★★	★
POLYESTER	★★★	★★★	★★★	★★★	★★

CHAPTER 2

YARN

Yarn is the essential
medium in knitting,
transforming raw fibers
into creative possibilities.
Its weight, twist, and
ply not only influence a
knit's structure but also
its drape and feel, making
yarn selection pivotal
to successful knitting
outcomes.

2.1 KNITTING YARN

Yarn is made up of strands of natural, man-made or regenerated fibers or filaments. Smoothness, hand feel, luster and evenness are considered when comparing staple and filament yarns. These characteristics are determined by the length, type, and quality of fibers used.

2.1.1 STAPLE VS FILAMENT YARN

	STAPLE OR SPUN YARN Short-staple fibers	FILAMENT YARN Continuous-filament fibers can be made from a single filament (monofilament) or many filaments (multifilament)

COMMON COMPOSITION	▪ Animal fibers ▪ Plant fibers ▪ Man-made spun fibers ▪ Spun silk	▪ Man-made filament fibers ▪ Silk
TEXTURE	Hairy due to fiber length	Smooth in general
HANDLE	Lofty and bulky	Compact
LUSTER	Tends to be matte; luster depends on fiber length; longer staples are more lustrous in general	Continuous fiber provides a higher degree of luster
EVENNESS	Uneven	Even
SPINNING PRODUCTION SYSTEM	Ring spinning / mule spinning	Wet spinning / dry spinning / melt spinning
GENERAL SPINNING PROCESS	Twisted or spun to hold yarns together	A solution is poured through a spinneret; in the case of silk, strands are twisted together to form yarn

2.1.2
SPINNING SYSTEMS

 COTTON SPINNING SYSTEM

CARDING

Carding is a low-cost yarn production process that creates fuzzy yarn.

COMBING

This is a more expensive production process; it creates a smoother, softer yarn. Combing includes carding and additional processes that produce more waste.

	CARDING	COMBING
FIBER	Cotton, waste silk, silk noil, bast, hair or wool, and synthetic spun	Fine cotton, and all fibers after carding
LENGTH OF FIBER	Short, medium, and long	Long staple
CHARACTERISTICS	■ Non-uniform ■ Usually coarser to the touch ■ Shrinks easily	■ Straight and aligned ■ Soft and smooth to the touch ■ Lustrous in appearance

WOOL / ANIMAL SPINNING SYSTEM

WOOLEN

Woolen threads are uneven yarn made from carded and uneven wool fibers.

WORSTED

Worsted yarns are combed wool yarns made from longer wool fibers.

	WOOLEN	WORSTED
LENGTH OF FIBER	25.4-76.2mm: short	76.2mm or above: long staple
CHARACTERISTICS	■ Bulky and uneven ■ Slackly twisted ■ Soft and hairy	■ Fine and even ■ Tightly twisted ■ Smooth, with little fuzz

2.1.3
STAPLE YARN SPINNING

RING SPINNING

- Silvers are drafted into rovings and twisted into yarns before being wound onto the bobbin
- Tight twist
- Fine – Superfine
- Suitable for all
- Staple fibers

MULE SPINNING

- Carded fibers are rubbed together without drafting, and spun on a mule-type machine that has no drafting roller, mirroring the processing pattern of hand-spinning
- Loose twist
- Coarse – Fine
- Lambswool, Shetland wool, cashmere, alpaca

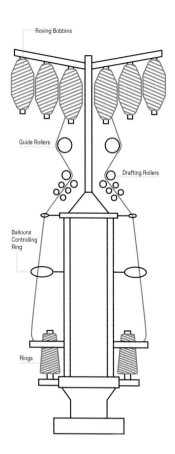

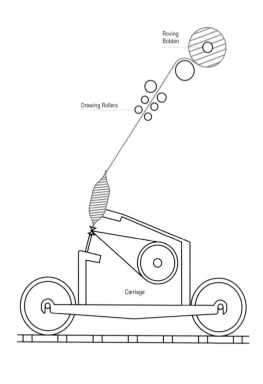

2.1.4
FILAMENT YARN SPINNING

WET SPINNING

- Polymers are dissolved in solvent and extruded directly into a liquid bath
- Viscose rayon, acrylic, aramid, spandex
- Toxic production process
- Slow production rate

DRY SPINNING

- Polymers are dissolved in a volatile solvent that evaporates when extruded
- Acetate, acrylic
- Toxic production process; risk of explosion
- Fast production rate

MELT SPINNING

- Polymer granules are melted and then extruded through the spinneret
- Polyester, nylon
- Non-toxic production process
- Fastest production rate

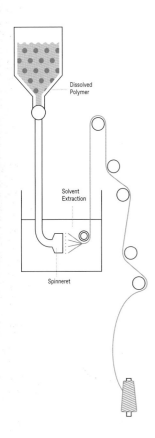

Dissolved Polymer

Solvent Extraction

Spinneret

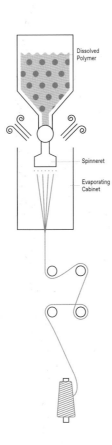

Dissolved Polymer

Spinneret

Evaporating Cabinet

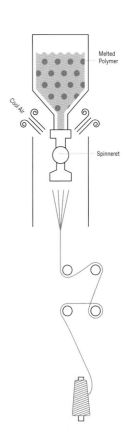

Melted Polymer

Cool Air

Spinneret

2.1.5
YARN
TWIST

■
DIRECTION

The direction of twist affects the reflection of light and the appearance of a fabric. Twist directions are described as either "S" or "Z". Most spun yarn has a "Z" twist. Twist direction does not influence the properties of single yarns, and the ply twist direction is generally the opposite of the twist direction of the yarn.

Z TWIST
Thread appears to move upwards toward the right yarn

S TWIST
Thread appears to move upwards toward the left yarn

■
LEVEL

The twist level is determined by the number of turns present in a unit of yarn length. High-twist yarn has a higher number of twists within the same unit length when compared to low-twist yarn. The twist number determines the yarn's strength, elongation characteristics, and air permeability. Yarn used for weaving tends to have a high twist, resulting in smooth surfaces and higher lengthwise strength. Yarn used for knitting has a looser twist.

LOW TWIST
Used to make bulky, soft, and fuzzy fabrics

HIGH TWIST
Used to make smoother surfaces and denser fabrics

■
COMMON TWIST

Twist influences the handle and appearance of a knitted fabric and a single yarn.

TPI*	LEVEL	YARN OUTCOME	COMMON YARN TYPE
0.5-1	Low twist	■ Less elasticity ■ Remains the same strength	Filament
2-12	Soft twist	■ Softer and fluffier ■ More flexible ■ Increased strength	Spun
20-30	Hard twist (crepe twist)	■ Smoother ■ Firmer ■ Stronger	Filament and spun

*The common TPI – turns per inch or twists per inch – of knitting yarn is .5 to 30

2.2 YARN TYPES

2.2.1 YARN TYPES - THE BASICS

ROVING
Loose assemblage of fibers drawn or rubbed into yarn of a single strand, with very little twist.

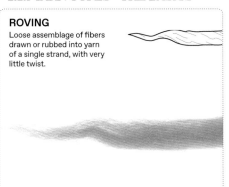

SINGLE / SINGLE-STRAND
Composed of fibers held together by twist, or filaments grouped together either with or without twist.

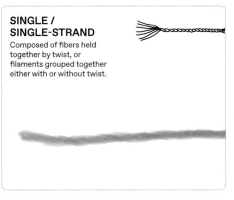

FOLDED / PLIED
Formed by twisting two or more single yarns (strands) together. It can be 2-ply, 3-ply, 4-ply, and so on.

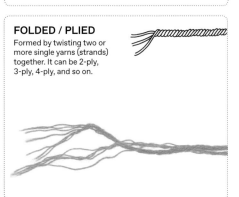

CABLED / CORD
Formed by twisting two or more plied yarns together.

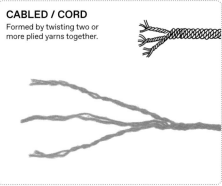

CABLED YARN STRUCTURE

A cabled yarn structure is broken into "single", "ply" and "cord".
E.g. 2/2/20Nm is a tier cord composed of two 1/20Nm yarn plied together, and two of these plied yarns twisted to form a cord. It is referred to 2/2/20, "two cord, two ply, twenties."

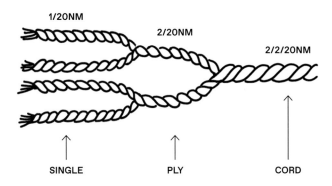

2.3

YARN COUNT & NUMBER

The "count" or "number" of a yarn is a numerical expression that defines its fineness. It indicates the yarn's weight-length ratio.

2.3.1 YARN COUNT SYSTEMS

	INDIRECT		DIRECT		
	The higher the count, the finer the yarn		The higher the count, the coarser the yarn		
	The lower the count, the coarser the yarn		The lower the count, the finer the yarn		
FIBER / YARN	Spun yarn other than cotton	Cotton & cotton-blend yarn	Continuous-filament yarn		
SYSTEM	Metric count	English cotton count	Denier	Tex	Decitex
SYMBOL	Nm	NeC / ECC / 'S	Td	Tt	dTex
FORMULA	$\dfrac{\text{LENGTH}}{\text{UNIT WEIGHT}}$		$\dfrac{\text{WEIGHT}}{\text{UNIT LENGTH}}$		
LENGTH UNIT	1000m	840yd	9000m	1000m	10,000m
MASS UNIT	1kg	1lb	1g	1g	1g
PRESENT FORMAT	Number of ply / count	Count / number of ply	Number/ strand	Number	Number
	e.g. a 10Nm single yarn: 1/10Nm a 10Nm double yarn: 2/10Nm	e.g. a 20NeC single yarn: 20/1Nec or 20'S/1 a 20NeC double yarn: 20/2Nec or 20'S/2	e.g. A 150-denier single yarn: 150Td or 150D a 24-strand 70-denier yarn: 70D24F	e.g. a 17 Tex single yarn: 17Tt	e.g. a 150 decitex single yarn: 150dTex

2.3.2
YARN COUNT CONVERSION

YARN CONVERSION FACTOR

METRIC COUNT (Nm)	ENGLISH COTTON COUNT (NeC/'S)	DENIER (Td/D)	TEX (Tt)	DECITEX (dTex)
	$NeC = \dfrac{Nm}{1.693}$	$Td = \dfrac{9000}{Nm}$	$Tt = \dfrac{1000}{Nm}$	$dTex = \dfrac{10{,}000}{Nm}$
$Nm = NeC \times 1.693$		$Td = \dfrac{5315}{NeC}$	$Tt = \dfrac{590.5}{NeC}$	$dTex = \dfrac{5905}{NeC}$
$Nm = \dfrac{9000}{Td}$	$NeC = \dfrac{5315}{Td}$		$Tt = \dfrac{Td}{9}$	$dTex = \dfrac{Td}{0.9}$
$Nm = \dfrac{1000}{Tt}$	$NeC = \dfrac{590.5}{Tt}$	$Td = \dfrac{Tt}{0.1111}$		$dTex = \dfrac{Tt}{0.1}$
$Nm = \dfrac{10000}{dTex}$	$NeC = \dfrac{5905}{dTex}$	$Td = \dfrac{dTex}{1.1111}$	$Tt = \dfrac{dTex}{10}$	

CONVERSION EXAMPLES

32S/2 100% cotton yarn in metric count:
= 2/(32 x 1.693) Nm
= 2/54 Nm

20/2Nec 55% acrylic 45% cotton yarn in metric count:
= 2/(20 x 1.693) Nm
= 2/34 Nm

300D 100% viscose yarn in metric count:
= 1/(9000 ÷ 300) Nm
= 1/30 Nm

2.3.3
COMMON USE YARN COUNT

SINGLE YARN

METRIC COUNT (Nm)	ENGLISH COTTON COUNT (NeC/'S)	DENIER (Td/D)
$\dfrac{\text{Total length in meters/kg}}{1000\text{m/kg}}$	$\dfrac{\text{Total length in yards/lb}}{840\text{yd/lb}}$	$\dfrac{\text{Total weight in grams} \times 9000\text{m}}{1\text{gm} \times \text{total length}}$

QUESTION
What is the yarn count of a single yarn that weighs 1,000g and has a length of 10km?

QUESTION
What is the yarn count of a single yarn that weighs 1lb and has a length of 16,800yd?

QUESTION
What is the yarn count of a single yarn that weighs 10g and has a length of 300m?

ANSWER

$\dfrac{10000\text{m/kg}}{1000\text{m/kg}}$

= 10Nm

ANSWER

$\dfrac{16800\text{yd/lb}}{840\text{yd/lb}}$

= 20Nec/'S

ANSWER

$\dfrac{10\text{g} \times 9000\text{m}}{1\text{gm} \times 300\text{m}}$

= 300Td/D

PLIED / MULTIFILAMENT YARN

For staple yarns, the number of plies should be indicated when giving counts for ply yarns. Whereas filament yarn is composed of a bundle of filaments, it is customary to give the number of filaments as well as denier.

METRIC COUNT (Nm)	ENGLISH COTTON COUNT (NeC/'S)	DENIER (Td/D)
Single yarn count / number of ply or filament		
QUESTION How to indicate two 20Nm single yarns that have been twisted together to form a yarn?	QUESTION How to indicate three 60'S single yarns that have been twisted together to form a yarn?	QUESTION How to indicate 150Td yarn composed of 40 filament fiber strands to form a yarn?
ANSWER 2 (plies) x 1/20	ANSWER 60/1 x 3 (plies)	ANSWER 150 Td x 40 (strands)
=2/20Nm * The thickness of 2/20Nm is equivalent to 1/10Nm (2/20 = 1/10)	= 60/3Nec or 60'S/3 *The thickness of 60'S/3 is equivalent to 20'S/1 (60/3 = 20/1)	= 150Td/40f or 150/40 *The filament fiber strands do not affect the thickness of the yarn

2.3.4
RESULTANT COUNT

Multiple strands of yarn are often used together in knitting. Resultant count calculates the yarn's effective thickness, provides a standard comparison of yarn thickness and helps knitters determine machine gauge.

ENDS: The term "ends" in knitting refers to the number of yarns used together in knitting. If the product is knitted with two cones of yarn, it is referred to as "2 ends".

METRIC COUNT (Nm)	ENGLISH COTTON COUNT (NeC/'S)	DENIER (Td/D)
$$\dfrac{\text{Piled yarn count}}{\text{Number of ends x number of ply}}$$		Plied yarn count x number of ends x number of ply
QUESTION What is the resultant count of 2 ends of 2/20 Nm yarns?	QUESTION What is the resultant count of 3 ends of 24/2 NeC yarns?	QUESTION What is the resultant count of 2 ends of 120Td x 2
ANSWER $$\dfrac{20}{2 \times 2} = 5$$	ANSWER $$\dfrac{24}{3 \times 2} = 4$$	ANSWER 120 x 2 x 2 = 480
The resultant count: = 1/5 Nm	The resultant count: = 4/1 NeC or 4'S/1	The resultant count: = 480Td or 480D

2.3.5
YARN OF DIFFERENT CONTENT

Yarns of different fiber content are often knitted together in a garment, such as 1 end of 100% wool yarn (measured in Nm) with 1 end of 100% polyester yarn (measured in Td). Calculating the resultant count of these yarns necessitates a conversion between the different counting systems.

QUESTION

What is the resultant count of a garment knitted with 1 end of 1/16Nm 100% wool yarn (Yarn A) and 1 end of 300Td 100% viscose yarn (Yarn B)?

QUESTION

What is the resultant count of a garment knitted with 1 end of 20'S/2 100% cotton yarn (Yarn C) and 1 end of 70Td 100% nylon yarn (Yarn D)?

ANSWER

STEP 1	STEP 2	STEP 3
Convert Yarn A from 1/16Nm to Td:	The resultant yarn number:	The resultant yarn count (convert Td to Nm):
9000/16	562.5Td (Yarn A) + 300Td (Yarn B)	9000/862.5
= 562.5Td	= 862.5Td	= 10.43Nm

ANSWER

STEP 1	STEP 2	STEP 3
Convert Yarn C from 20S'/2 to Td: 20S'/2 = 10S'/1 (thickness equivalent)	The resultant yarn number:	The resultant yarn count (convert Td to Nm):
5315/10	531.5Td (Yarn C) + 70Td (Yarn D)	9000/601.5
= 531.5Td	= 601.5Td	= 14.96Nm

2.3.6
MACHINE GAUGE FOR APPLICABLE YARN COUNT

Machine gauge refers to the number of knitting needles per inch in a knitting machine. Machine gauges for knitting typically range from 3.5G to 18G.

GAUGE	Nm (Min)	Nm (Avg)	Nm (Max)	
18G	29.5	33.8	40.5*	FINE GAUGE
16G	23.3	26.7	32*	
14G	17.8	20.4	24.5*	
12G	12	15	21*	
9G	7.36	8.5	10.13*	
7G	5.44	7	9.8	
5G	2.77	3.57	5	COARSE GAUGE
3.5G	1.53	1.88	2.45	

*Elastomeric yarn

2.4

YARN FINISHING

Finishing can be applied to yarn to create a special function or appearance.

2.4.1
APPEARANCE

■ MERCERIZING

Mercerization enhances the luster, color yield, and strength of cellulosic yarn. The yarn or fabric is immersed in a sodium hydroxide bath, then neutralized in acid. The fibers permanently swell and stretch through the process resulting in a smooth surface that reflects light more effectively.

FIBER CROSS-SECTION VIEW

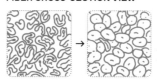

FIBER LONGITUDINAL VIEW

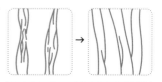

■ GASSING & SINGEING

Gassing and singeing removes protruding fibers or fuzz on yarns by passing it through gas flames or heated copper plates, or infrared radiation (for singeing). This burns off any excess fibers, resulting in a smoother surface. Yarns treated in this way are referred to as "gassed yarn" or, in the case of worsted yarn, "genapped yarn".

2.4.2
FUNCTION

■ UV PROTECTION

Additives are applied during the filament-spinning process to absorb or scatter UV rays to protect skin from sunburn and skin cancer.

UPF	GRADE	CLASSIFICATION
40-50, 50+	A	Excellent
25-39	B	Very good
15-24	C	Good

■ MOISTURE WICKING

The structure of moisture-wicking yarns allows moisture to move through the fabric. Capillary action allows sweat to wick away from the body and evaporate.

REGULAR YARN
A normal yarn is
round in shape

WICKING YARN
Wicking yarns come in various shapes;
cross-shaped is the most common

ANTI-PILLING

Anti-pilling treatment is applied to yarn to prevent the formation of fuzzy balls caused by friction. Short fibers, loose fibers and blended fibers are more likely to pill.

TYPES OF ANTI-PILLING TREATMENTS:

Reducing static electricity via a co-polymerization modification method

Lowering the average molecular weight of polymers

Applying anti-pilling agents (such as amide polymers and non-ionic polyurethane resins)

Applying anti-pilling coating

SHRINK RESISTANCE

This prevents dimensional changes in the fabric or garment during the manufacturing process. A shrink-resist treatment is usually applied on natural fibers.

EXAMPLES OF SHRINK RESISTANCE TREATMENT

WOOL AND ANIMAL FIBERS
Chlorination treatment
→ smooths the scales of the fiber and reduces inter-fiber friction, which minimizes the fibers' tendency to felt and shrink when washed.

COTTON AND NATURAL FIBERS
Fluorocarbon resin emulsion
→ coats the fiber with a hydrophobic layer that reduces fiber swelling and distortion, thus preventing shrinkage during washing.

ANTI-BACTERIAL / ANTI-MICROBIAL

Treatents can be applied to inhibit the growth and reproduction of bacteria and other microorganisms. This can offer several benefits:

ODOR CONTROL
Prevent or reduce odors caused by metabolic processes of bacteria and fungi.

DURABILITY
Enhance longevity of natural material by avoiding weakening of material cuased by microorganisms.

MAINTAIN APPEARANCE
Prevent stains and discoloration caused by pigments produced by bacteria and fungi.

HYGIENE & HEALTH
Reduce risk of infections, skin irritations, and allergies caused by microorganisms.

FACT: Anti-microbial agent can be applied in different yarn spnning methods:

On fibers' surface

In spinning solvent
(for wet & melt spinning)

In liquid bath (wet spinning) or spinning finishes (melt spinning)

In sheath polymer to produce sheath core fibers

2.5

TYPES OF FANCY YARN

2.5.1
COLORED YARN

HEATHER / INGRAIN
A yarn made from fibers of two or more colors.

MELANGE
A blended or unblended yarn spun from tops combined with raw white fibers.

MARL
A single yarn produced from rovings of two different colors.

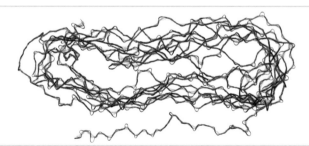

TWIST
A yarn comprising two single ends of different colors twisted together, the single ends being either a solid color or a mixture.

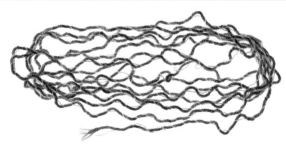

2.5.2
NOVELTY & TEXTURED YARN

AIR JET
Also called fasciated yarn; a layer of fiber is wound around a core of parallel fibers.

BOUCLÉ
A yarn made from loops of similar size. A crimped shape is formed by heat-setting knitted fabric, then unraveling the yarn.

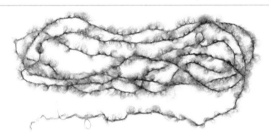

CHENILLE
Chenille is French for "caterpillar;" chenille yarn is made by placing short lengths of yarn between two long core yarns. It is then twisted, producing a soft, fuzzy strand.

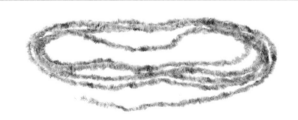

CORE SPUN
A central yarn wrapped in a web of twisted fiber.

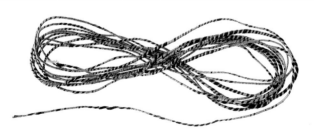

ECCENTRIC

A twisted core with an effect yarn wrapped with compound yarn to produce a wavy surface.

FEATHER

Also called eyelash yarn, feather yarn is different from chenille; long strands of decorative yarn are wrapped around the core yarn.

FLAKE

A variation on slub yarn; small clumps of puffy, short staple fibers are inserted at intervals between long staple fibers, or binder yarns.

GIMP

A gimp is a compound yarn consisting of a twisted core with an effect yarn wrapped around it to produce wavy projections on its surface.

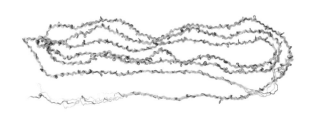

KNOP / KNOT / NUB

A ply yarn with knobs that is often made by twisting one ply faster than another.

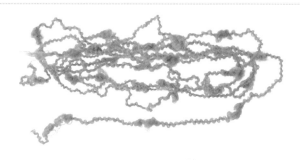

LOOP

Yarn that is twisted to form loops or curls.

NEP

A single or plied novelty yarn with small neps added intentionally during the carding process.

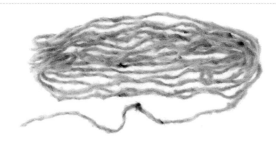

CRÊPE

A hard-twist yarn with a considerably larger number of turns per unit length than ordinary yarn.

PAPER

A wood pulp-made yarn usually cut into strips and twisted into yarn form.

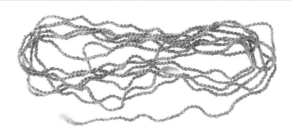

SLUB

Yarn that is spun irregularly in terms of length and diameter, resulting in intermittent lumps.

SNARL

Made by a similar method to loop yarn, snarl yarn has the effect of a lively, high-twist yarn and a somewhat large degree of overfeed.

SPIRAL

A coarse yarn is wound around a fine yarn, giving it a spiral effect.

STRIPE

Similar to knop yarn, stripe yarn has elongated knops.

STUFFING BOX

Fiber is fed into a tubular yarn, creating a soft, puffy hand feel.

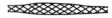

TAPE / RIBBON

A flat yarn made by various processes including knitting, crocheting or weaving.

TUBULAR

Also called ribbon yarn, tubular yarn is a flat yarn made in a circular, seamless form.

TWEED

Consists of different-colored singles from woolen yarns in a range of weights and qualities.

METALLIC

This yarn has a shiny appearance, and is often twisted with other fibers for a decorative effect.

CHAPTER 3

PRINCIPLES OF KNITTING

Knitting is a method of constructing fabric by intermeshing a series of loops of one or more yarns. Different techniques and stitch patterns, as well as yarn tension and needle size, determine the final fabric structure and properties.

3.1

KNITTING PRINCIPLES

Knitting, through interlocking yarn loops, achieves remarkable elasticity and recovery. The intricate variations in stitching, structural design, and knitting methods allow for a vast array of textures, patterns, and functional properties in garments and textiles.

3.1.1
WALES & COURSES

■
WALES
Vertical columns of stitches and vertical chains of loops.

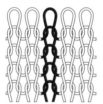

Weft-knitted fabric: Wale

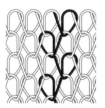

Warp-knitted fabric: Wale

■
COURSES
Horizontal rows of stitches, along with rows of loops or stitches, run across the knitted fabric.

Weft-knitted fabric: Course

Warp-knitted fabric: Course

■
KNITTING DIRECTION
In weft knitting, the entire fabric is usually produced from a single yarn, with the wales and courses running roughly perpendicular. In warp knitting, the wales and courses run roughly parallel.

■
ELASTICITY
The course-wise extension is approximately twice that of the wale-wise extension.

3.1.2
KNITTING METHODS COMPARISON

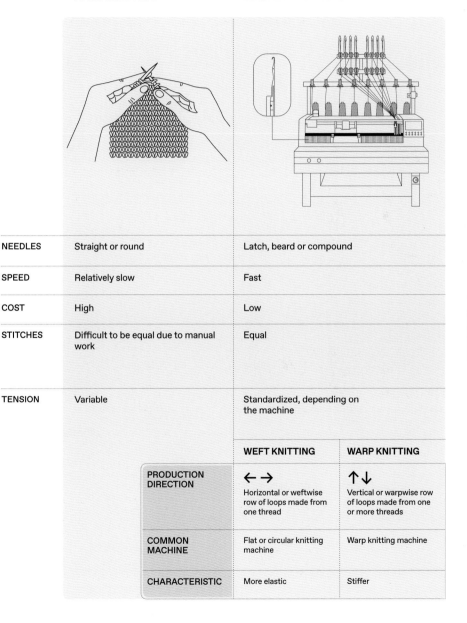

	HAND KNITTING	MACHINE KNITTING	
NEEDLES	Straight or round	Latch, beard or compound	
SPEED	Relatively slow	Fast	
COST	High	Low	
STITCHES	Difficult to be equal due to manual work	Equal	
TENSION	Variable	Standardized, depending on the machine	

		WEFT KNITTING	WARP KNITTING
	PRODUCTION DIRECTION	← → Horizontal or weftwise row of loops made from one thread	↑↓ Vertical or warpwise row of loops made from one or more threads
	COMMON MACHINE	Flat or circular knitting machine	Warp knitting machine
	CHARACTERISTIC	More elastic	Stiffer

3.2 KNITTING SYMBOLS

LOOP DIAGRAM

Symbols used to represent stitches

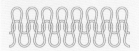

YARN PATH DIAGRAM

Symbols used to represent needles

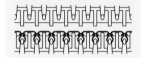

NOTATION

Symbols used to represent structural elements in knit pattern

3.2.1 NOTATION SYMBOLS

Knit (technical face)	Purl (technical back)	Tuck	Miss	Full needles
Filling in	Tubular	Slip stitch	Float stitch	Face left racking
Face right racking	Right over cross	Left over cross	Face right widening	Face left widening
Face right narrowing	Face left narrowing	Back right narrowing	Back left narrowing	Face three stitches in one
Back three stitches in one	Transfer left stitch to the right needle	Transfer right stitch to the left needle	Back right widening	Back left widening

3.3 STITCH DENSITY

Stitch density is required for the calculation of the knitting scheme. Taking stitch measurements after washing is believed to be more reliable than before washing; laundering the fabric will relax the tension. Normally, a loose-tension fabric is lighter than a dense fabric of the same specification.

$$\text{Number of stitches per unit} = \text{Number of courses per unit} \times \text{Number of wales per unit}$$

*The higher number of stitches, the higher the stitch density.

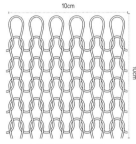

LOOSE TENSION

NORMAL TENSION

TIGHT TENSION

HOW TO CHECK IF FABRIC IS TOO TIGHT OR TOO LOOSE

Manually stretch the fabric lengthwise to its limit and measure the dimension of 10 wales. Compare it to the desired dimension to establish whether the fabric is too loose, too tight, or adequate.

This simple method is widely used in the industry. However, it is not scientific, and the accuracy is affected by individual's stretch strength.

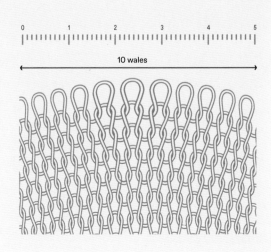

3.4

STITCHES & TECHNIQUES

3.4.1
LOOPS

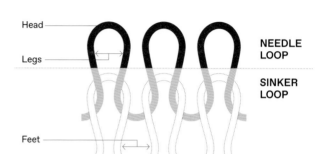

Head — NEEDLE LOOP

Legs

SINKER LOOP

Feet

3.4.2
BASIC STITCHES

KNIT
KNIT STITCH (TECHNICAL FACE)
In this V-shaped stitch, the feet are below the head of the preceding stitch.

PURL STITCH (TECHNICAL BACK)

The legs are below and the feet are above the head of the preceding stitch.

TUCK
A loop without casting off the previous stitch; a tuck stitch consists of a held loop and a tuck loop in the same course.

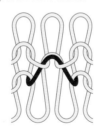

MISS
A miss connects two loops without forming a new loop in the same course.

SLIP STITCH (SKIP BEHIND)

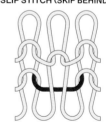

FLOAT STITCH (SKIP FRONT)

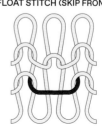

3.4.3
ADVANCED STITCHES

TRANSFER

Transfers a loop from one needle to another. Commonly used to generate holes or produce structural effects and cables.

SPREAD / FILLING IN / HALF TRANSFER

This is a widening process, knitting a new loop on the empty needle. Widely used in seamless knitting.

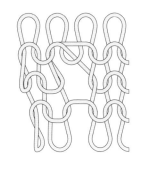

NARROWING

Moving loops at the selvage is a technique used to narrow a piece of fabric. A "fashioning mark" is created at the point where two wales merge into one, and it is slightly thicker than the surrounding fabric.

3.4.4
OTHER KNITTING TECHNIQUES

PLATING

Knitting two (or more) yarns separately by different yarn carriers at almost the same time. Plated loops are composed of yarns to achieve double-faced colors or patterns by placing the second yarn under the first yarn.

Face Yarn ■ Base Yarn

RACKING

In racking, a lateral movement of the needle-bed on a flat knitting machine results in a zigzag pattern.

STRIPING

Different yarn carriers, working across the full knitting width, achieve horizontal stripes.

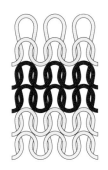

3.5

TYPES OF
KNITTED GARMENTS

ALL CUT

Garment pieces are cut from
fabric, then sewn together.

Collars

FULLY FASHIONED

Pieces of the garment are
knitted into the exact shape
required, then joined using a
dial-linking machine.

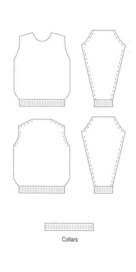

Collars

SEAMLESS

Garments are produced as
one piece. Sometimes the
beginning and the end of the
garment is joined.

ADVANTAGES
■ Higher production rate
■ Low-cost fabric without
  progressive narrowing

DISADVANTAGES
■ Labor intensive
■ Higher fabric waste
■ Lack of seam elasticity

ADVANTAGES
■ Little or no cutting waste
■ Effective production

DISADVANTAGES
■ Experienced technicians
  are required

ADVANTAGES
■ Low labor costs
■ Minimum waste
■ Saves linking time

DISADVANTAGES
■ Experienced technicians
  are required
■ High machine costs,
  commonly used for bulk
  orders with simple designs

3.6 KNITTING MACHINE TERMS

LATCH NEEDLES

The specially designed needles used in knitting machines, featuring a hook and a latch that opens and closes to form stitches.

CARRIAGE

The part of the knitting machine that holds the yarn and forms the stitches as it moves across the needles. Also called the "slider" or "knitter."

NEEDLE BED

The flat surface of the knitting machine where the latch needles are mounted. It holds the needles in a linear arrangement.

GATING

The needlebed arrangement in a knitting machine, which need to be adjusted based on stitch structure.

RIB GATING

A configuration where needles on both the front and back beds of the machine are arranged in alternating order on a double bed knitting machine.

INTERLOCK GATING

A configuration where needles on the front and back beds are set on in opposed arrangement on a double bed knitting machine.

GAUGE

Often known as "cut" in the US, gauge is an expression used to describe the needle spacing. Due to origins of different machine types, the gauge can be expressed in number of stitches per inch.

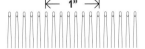

CASTING ON

Refers to the process of initializing the first row of stitches. It is done by positioning the yarn on the needles of the machine's frame before starting the knitting process.

CASTING OFF

Refers to the process of finalizing the knitted work by removing the loops from the active needles when no yarn is present. It is done by stopping feeding yarn to the needles.

BINDING OFF

Refers to the process of securing the final row of stitches to prevent them from unraveling. It's achieved by knitting two stitches, then passing the first stitch over the second. This process is repeated until all stitches are secured.

DRAW THREAD

A draw thread is introduced in the form of one row of loops during knitting; on removal, it permits the separation of fabrics that are knitted in a succession of connected units.

RAVEL COURSE
(ROVING COURSE / HAND HOLD / WASTE COURSE)

These additional courses are used either as protective courses or to facilitate handling in subsequent operations in the manufacture of knitted fabric. These courses are removed afterward.

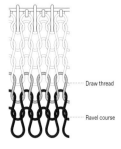

Draw thread

Ravel course

3.7

TYPES OF KNITTING MACHINES

SINGLE FLATBED MACHINE

- Needles are mounted on a single needle bed
- Needles are operated by cams mounted in a carriage
- Cam carriage is traversed by hand
- Gauge: 1 ½ - 7 G

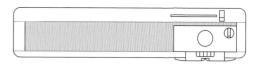

APPLICATION

- Commonly used for complex color intarsia.

V-BED FLAT MACHINE / HAND FLAT MACHINE

- Needles are mounted on two beds in an inverted V formation
- Needles are operated by cams in a reciprocating carriage
- Cam carriage is traversed by hand
- Gauge: 1 ½ - 16 G

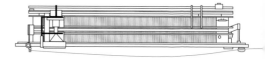

APPLICATION

- Can produce most knit structures.
- Commonly used for fully fashioned garments and knit swatches.

SEAMLESS KNITTING / 3-D KNITTING MACHINE

- 4-5 needle beds are equipped
- Cam carriage is traversed automatically
- Needles are operated by cams
- Gauge: 7 - 18 G

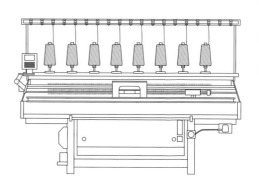

APPLICATION

- Used to produce seamless garments.

ELECTRONIC FLAT MACHINE

- Needles are mounted on 2 beds opposed in an inverted V formation
- Needles are operated by cams in a reciprocating carriage
- Cam carriage is traversed automatically
- Gauge: 1 ½ - 18 G

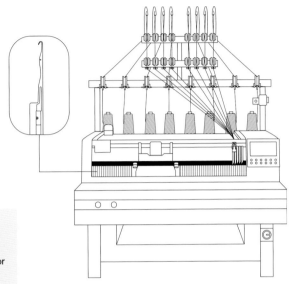

APPLICATION

- Can produce most knit structures.
- Widely used for fully fashioned garments and occasionally used for seamless accessories.

CIRCULAR MACHINE

- Needles are mounted on revolving cylinders
- Operated by revolving cylinders and stationary cams
- Gauge: 16 - 32 G

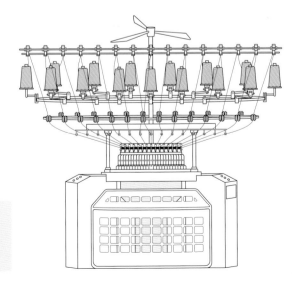

APPLICATION

- Commonly used for knit fabric to make cut and sewn knit items such as T-shirts or sweatshirts.

CHAPTER 4

KNITTING STRUCTURES & PATTERNS

The world of knitting structures and patterns offers endless possibilities for creative expression. By experimenting with different stitches and combinations, unique textures and designs emerge, each contributing to the distinct appearance and function of the knitted piece.

JERSEY

Jersey, also known as plain knit, is the fastest basic form of knitting. It is characterized by a smooth flat surface and textured purl back. It is lightweight with some degree of stretch.

LIGHTWEIGHT

Lightweight compared to other knits, and the fastest to produce.

CURLING

Fabric tends to curl toward the front at the ends and toward the back at the sides.

LADDERING

Can ladder from both the first and the last knitted course.

LOOP DIAGRAM

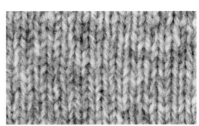

FRONT: Classic V-shaped stitches

BACK: Semicircular loops

STORY

Coco Chanel's innovative use of jersey, a material traditionally confined to undergarments and sportswear, marked a profound shift in women's fashion. By incorporating this flexible, comfortable fabric into her collections, she not only challenged fashion norms, but also significantly enhanced womens' mobility and comfort.

GATING SETTING

1 set of needle bed.

NOTATION

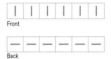

Front

Back

YARN PATH DIAGRAM

Single course repeat structure, all-needle knit on one needle bed.

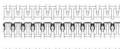

COMMON APPLICATIONS

T-shirts

Baby clothes

Underwear

Sweaters

Dresses

Fine cardigans

DOUBLE JERSEY

Double jersey is also called plain rib, full-needle rib, or 1x1 all-needle rib. It is a compact double-faced jersey fabric with two smooth sides, offering more structure and stability than single jersey.

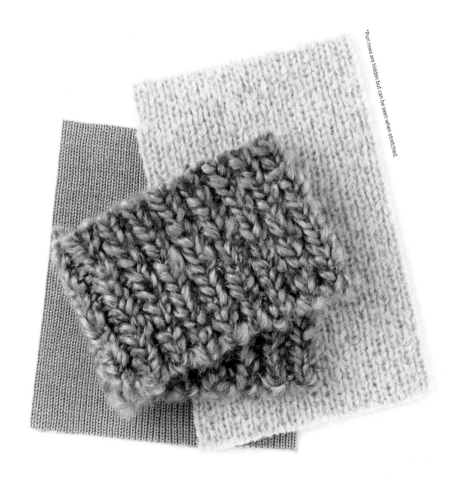

*Purl rows are hidden but can be seen when stretched.

THICKER & HEAVIER

The thickness and weight of double jersey are twice that of 1x1 rib fabric.

STABLE STRUCTURE

Stable and a more compact structure than single jersey and interlock.

REVERSIBLE

A reversible knitted fabric that appears the same on both sides.

LOOP DIAGRAM

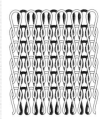

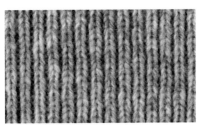

FRONT: Classic V-shaped stitches

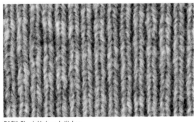

BACK: Classic V-shaped stitches

STORY

Double knit was popular during the 1970s for pants, socks, tops and even suits. It is often made from polyester; the iconic '70s "leisure suit" was polyester double-knit jersey.

GATING SETTING   2 sets of needle beds in rib gating.

NOTATION

YARN PATH DIAGRAM

Single course repeat structure, all-needle knit on both beds in rib gating.

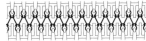

COMMON
APPLICATIONS

Underwear

Sportswear

Sweaters

Cardigans

Skirts

Collars

RIB

Rib is double-faced, with distinct vertical ridges on both sides. It is highly elastic in the crosswise direction with excellent shape retention.

REVERSIBLE
Reversible when the number of knit and purl stitches are equal.

LAY FLAT
Edges of rib do not curl.

HIGH ELASTICITY
Excellent widthwise elasticity. Elasticity decreases when the number of wales in each rib increases.

GATING SETTING
2 sets of needle beds in rib or interlock gating, depends on the knit structure required.

KNITTING TIPS

Apply transfer needle techniques to create various rib patterns.

COMMON
APPLICATIONS

 Sweaters

 Scarves

 Hats

 Socks

 Collars

 Neckbands

 Cuffs & hems

 Waistbands

RIB
VARIATION °1

1×1 RIB
1×1 rib is also called half-gauge rib or English rib.

LOOP DIAGRAM

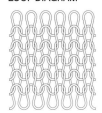

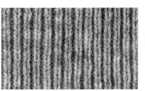

FRONT: Alternating knit and purl stitches

BACK: Alternating knit and purl stitches

GATING SETTING
Two sets of needles in interlock gating.

NOTATION

YARN PATH DIAGRAM

By aligning 1 active needle and 1 inactive needle, repeat the arrangement in both beds in interlock gating.

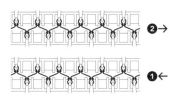

2×2 RIB

2x2 rib is also called Swiss rib. Two methods for producing 2x2 ribs on knitting machines are 2-in 1-out and 2-in 2-out.

RIB
VARIATION °2

2-IN 1-OUT NEEDLE SET OUT

2-in 1-out needle set produces tighter and more elastic fabric than 2-in 2-out needle set, often applied to waistband, hem and cuff. It is a more common option for 2x2 rib.

LOOP DIAGRAM

FRONT: Two wales of face loops alternate with two wales of back loops.

BACK: Two wales of face loops alternate with two wales of back loops.

GATING SETTING

2 sets of needle beds in rib gating.

NOTATION

$$- \ + \ | \ - \ + \ |$$

YARN PATH DIAGRAM

By aligning 2 active needles and 1 inactive needle, repeat the arrangement in both beds in rib gating.

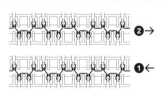

RIB VARIATION °3

2-IN 2-OUT NEEDLE SET OUT

It has a looser structure than 2-in 1-out and the width is broader (with the same number of needles). Usually used when a looser body, hem and cuff is preferred.

LOOP DIAGRAM

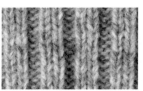

FRONT: Two wales of face loops alternate with two wales of back loops

BACK: Two wales of face loops alternate with two wales of back loops

GATING SETTING

2 sets of needle beds in interlock gating.

NOTATION

YARN PATH DIAGRAM

By aligning 2 active needles and 2 inactive needles, repeat the arrangement in both beds in interlock gating.

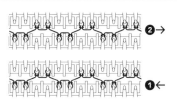

SIMPLE RIB

Also called "narrow rib." Single-rib wale with any number of consecutive plain wales, such as 3x1, 4x1.

3X1 RIB

3X1 RIB (BACK)

4X1 RIB

6X1 RIB

KNITTING
STITCH
COMBINA-
TIONS °2

BROAD RIB

The broad-rib structures may have any number of consecutive rib wales such as 6x3 (Derby rib) or 10x2.

3X3 RIB　　　　　　　　**6X6 RIB**

KNITTING
STITCH
COMBINA-
TIONS °3

MULTIPLE RIB

A combination of any number of consecutive rib wales. Normally 2-4 groups of wales as a repeat.

TUBULAR

A seamless, cylindrical knit structure, prized for its structural stability and resilience. Often used for trims, collars and cuffs in knitwear.

THICKER & HEAVIER
A thick fabric due to double layers.

STABLE STRUCTURE
Stable structure. Gives a clear and neat start to the border.

REVERSIBLE
A reversible double-faced fabric.

LOOP DIAGRAM

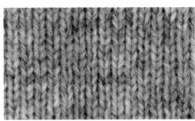

FRONT: Classic V-shaped stitches

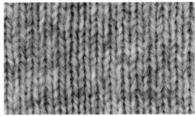

BACK: Classic V-shaped stitches

STORY

Tubular knitting comes in two forms: the tubular welt, a seamless, circular knit structure, and the split welt, with its distinct open tube structure, offering flat, open edges, often used in creating neat hemming or decorative elements on garments.

Split welt

Tubular welt

GATING SETTING

2 sets of needles in rib or interlock gating, depends on the knit structure required.

NOTATION

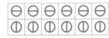

YARN PATH DIAGRAM

All-needle knit on front and back, alternately.

 **2 →**

STEP 2: All-needle knit on front bed.

 **1 ←**

STEP 1: All-needle knit on back bed.

COMMON APPLICATIONS

 Neckbands

 Cuffs & hems

 Plackets

OTTOMAN

Ottoman is also known as roll welt, English welt, and ripple. Features a distinct horizontal cord pattern, created by selective knitting and missing at the back of the welt.

THICKER & HEAVIER
The ripples on fabric giving thickness to the fabric.

LOW ELASTICITY
The ottoman structure is less elastic.

IRREVERSIBLE
Not reversible; ripples on one side.

LOOP DIAGRAM

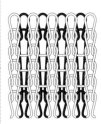

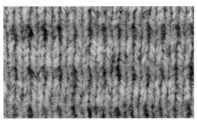

FRONT: Classic V-shaped stitches with rippled effect

BACK: Long V shape (long held loops)

GATING SETTING
2 sets of needles in rib gating.

NOTATION

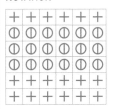

KNITTING TIPS
The rippled effect depends on the number of all-needle knit courses on the front bed.

YARN PATH DIAGRAM

A rib-based structure starts with 1x1 all-needle rib and is followed by all-needle knit continuously, normally from 2 to 4 courses on the front bed and none on the back bed, and ending with a 1x1 all-needle rib.

Ripple

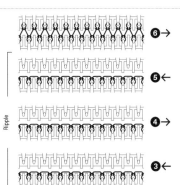

6 →
5 ←
4 →
3 ←
2 →
1 ←

STEP 1, 2, 6: 1x1 all-needle rib.

STEP 3, 4, 5: One set of needles knits continuously to form the face, while the other set of needles is selected to either knit or miss.

COMMON APPLICATIONS

Sweaters

Tops

Dresses

HALF MILANO

Half Milano, also known as semi-double knit, is an imbalanced rib-based jersey-like structure, widely used for plackets.

* Technical back (Commonly used as front)

THICKER & HEAVIER
Thicker than a single jersey due to rib base structure.

LADDERING
Can ladder from the last knitted course, but not from the first knitted course.

LAY FLAT
No rolling tendency due to the balanced structure.

CURLING
Slight curling due to imbalanced structure, but higher stability compared to jersey.

LOOP DIAGRAM

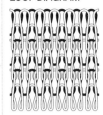

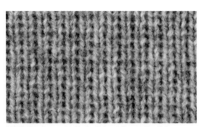

FRONT: A "single-course face" having the long-held course; long V shape.

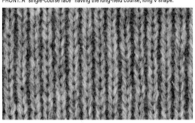

BACK: A "double-course face;" contains two courses in one repeat; V shape.

GATING SETTING

2 sets of needles in rib gating.

NOTATION

YARN PATH DIAGRAM

A rib-based structure, repeating a row of 1x1 all-needle rib and a row of jersey knit.

STEP 2: All needles on back bed.

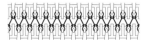
STEP 1: 1x1 all-needle rib.

COMMON APPLICATIONS

Sweaters

Cardigans

Scarves

Plackets

FULL MILANO

Full Milano, also known as double knit, is a double-faced, compact knit with a smooth surface. It is high in density, offering great stability, durability, and less elasticity.

STABLE STRUCTURE
Greater dimensional stability than half milano due to the repeat tubular knit.

LAY FLAT
Does not curl due to balanced structure.

REVERSIBLE
A reversible double-faced fabric.

LADDERING
Can ladder only from the last knitted course, but not from the first course.

LOOP DIAGRAM

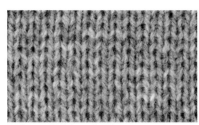

FRONT: 1 course of big V + 1 course of small V

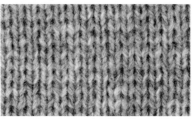

BACK: 1 course of big V + 1 course of small V

GATING SETTING

2 sets of needles in rib gating.

NOTATION

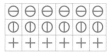

YARN PATH DIAGRAM

A 3-course repeat 1x1 all-needle rib followed by a repeat of tubular knit.

STEP 1: 1x1 all-needle rib.
STEPS 2-3: 1 repeat of tubular knit.

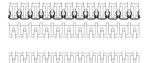

COMMON APPLICATIONS

Outerwear

Cardigans

Dresses

Pants

Skirts

PONTE DI ROMA

Ponte di roma is a double-knit interlock-based construction combining tubular and interlock structure. This compact knit offers stability and firmness with subtle horizontal ridges.

LOW ELASTICITY

Tubular course reduces widthwise elasticity.

STABLE STRUCTURE

More stable structure than plain interlock; can be sewn and cut easily.

REVERSIBLE

A double-face reversible knit due to its balanced tubular and interlock structure.

LOOP DIAGRAM

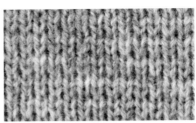

FRONT: 1 course of small V + 2 courses of big V

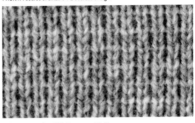

BACK: 1 course of small V + 2 courses of big V

STORY

Ponte di Roma, often associated with Rome, indeed translates to "Roman Bridge" from Italian. Its name is thought to be inspired by the fabric's structural characteristics, which metaphorically resemble the sturdy, arched construction of ancient Roman bridges.

GATING SETTING

2 sets of needles in interlock gating.

NOTATION

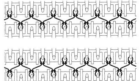

YARN PATH DIAGRAM

Alternately repeating tubular (step 1 + 2) and interlock (step 3 +4) structure.

 4→

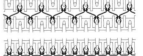 **3**←

 **2**→

 **1**←

COMMON APPLICATIONS

Outerwears

Cardigans

Dresses

Pants

Skirts

HALF CARDIGAN

Half cardigans is also known as royal rib. It is a modified form of coarsely knitted rib fabric that offers a heavier structure and soft handle, often use in clothing requiring extra bulkiness.

THICKER & HEAVIER
Tends to be thick due to tuck loops at back; heavier in weight and bulkier in handle.

HIGH ELASTICITY
Good elasticity; good stretch, especially horizontally.

IRREVERSIBLE
Not reversible due to altering different knitting courses.

LADDERING
Can ladder only from the last knitted course, but not from the first course.

LOOP DIAGRAM

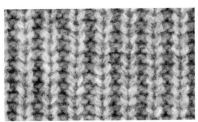

FRONT: Larger and rounder V shape

BACK: Smaller V shape

KNITTING TIPS

Apply transfer needle technique to create various half cardigan patterns.

GATING SETTING — 2 sets of needles in rib gating.

NOTATION

YARN PATH DIAGRAM

Alternatively knitting 1x1 all needles rib followed by all knit on front bed and tuck on back bed.

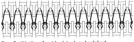
Step 2: all knit on front bed, tuck on back bed

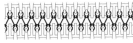

Step 1: 1x1 all needles rib

COMMON APPLICATIONS

 Sweaters

 Cardigans

 Cuffs & hems

 Neckbands

 Scarves

FULL CARDIGAN

Full cardigans, also called polka rib, is similar to half cardigan but reversible. It is usually knitted in a coarser gauge, making it ideal for cozy, warm garments.

* Fabric widthwise tends to spread outwards due to rib wales gaping apart.

THICKER & HEAVIER
Bulky and thick due to excessive tuck loop; feels thicker than half cardigan.

HIGH ELASTICITY
Great stretch, especially horizontally.

REVERSIBLE
Reversible; appears the same on both sides.

LADDERING
Can ladder only from the last knitted course, but not from the first course.

LOOP DIAGRAM

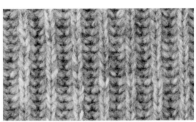

FRONT: Alternating a wale of knit and a wale of purl with ruck stitch

BACK: Same as front

GATING SETTING

2 sets of needles in rib gating.

NOTATION

YARN PATH DIAGRAM

A 2-course repeat 1x1 rib fabric. When one side is knitting, the opposite side is tucked and vice versa in the other course.

2 →

Step 2: Tuck on front bed, all knit on back bed

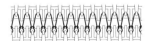

1 ←

Step 1: All knit on front bed, tuck on back bed

COMMON APPLICATIONS

Sweaters

Cardigans

Cuffs & hems

Neckbands

Scarves

INTERLOCK

Essentially two rib knits interlocked, creating a fabric with two smooth sides and a firm handle. It is often produced in a medium to fine gauge.

STABLE STRUCTURE
Stable structure, with a firm texture.

LAY FLAT
Does not curl due to balanced structure.

REVERSIBLE
Reversible; appears the same on both sides.

LADDERING
Can ladder only from the last knitted course, but not from the first course.

LOOP DIAGRAM

FRONT: Small V shape

BACK: Small V shape

GATING SETTING 2 sets of needles in interlock gating.

NOTATION

YARN PATH DIAGRAM

A repeat structure of alternative double 1x1 rib.

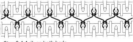 **2** →

Step 2: 1x1 rib on both beds

 **1** ←

Step 1: 1x1 rib on both beds

COMMON APPLICATIONS

Sweaters

Cardigans

T-shirts

Baby clothes

Sportswear

LINKS

Links is also known as links & links, purl, pearl, and garter stitch. This delicate pattern forms in a series of purl-stitch ridges and knit-stitch troughs, often used for borders and lace edges.

LAY FLAT
Does not curl due to balanced structure.

REVERSIBLE
Reversible and smooth; appears the same on both sides.

LADDERING
Can ladder only from the last knitted course, but not from the first course.

LOOP DIAGRAM

FRONT: Purl-stitch ridge and knit-stitch troughs

BACK: Purl-stitch ridge and knit-stitch troughs

GATING SETTING

2 sets of needles with interlock gating.

NOTATION

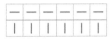

YARN PATH DIAGRAM

2-course repeat structure, alternating purl stitch on front and back, alternately.

2 →

Step 2: Needles need to be transferred from the front to the back bed, or the back to the front bed

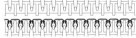

1 ←

Step 1: Alternating one course of knit stitch and one course of purl stitch

COMMON APPLICATIONS

Sweaters

Cardigans

Dresses

Scarves

Edgings

KNIT PURL TRANSFER

Knit and purl structure is a fancy variation of links, combining knit and purl stitches to create patterns and textures. It is often presented in a droplet-like pattern.

Seed stitch

Moss stitch

Double seed stitch

REVERSIBLE
Reversible; appears the same on both sides.

LAY FLAT
Does not curl due to balanced structure.

STABLE STRUCTURE
Stable due to double-knit structure.

GATING SETTING
2 sets of needles in interlock gating.

COMMON APPLICATIONS

Sweaters

Cardigans

Details & patterns

KNIT PURL
TRANSFER
VARIATION °1

MOSS STITCH

The most popular of the broken-rib-texture patterns, it is often used with cable patterns, and gives a pleasing nubby effect when used in large areas.

LOOP DIAGRAM

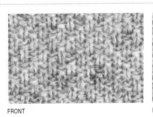

FRONT

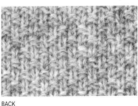

BACK

GATING SETTING

2 sets of needles in interlock gating.

NOTATION

—	|	—	|
—	|	—	|
|	—	|	—
|	—	|	—

YARN PATH DIAGRAM

Alternating 1 knit and 1 purl stitch in every 2 courses.

STEP 1 & 2: Alternating 1 knit and 1 purl
STEP 3 & 4 : Alternating 1 purl and 1 knit

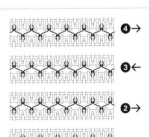

KNIT PURL
TRANSFER
VARIATION °2

SEED STITCH

Frequently used for borders and for a speckled texture effect.

LOOP DIAGRAM

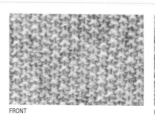

FRONT

BACK

GATING SETTING

2 sets of needles in interlock gating.

NOTATION

YARN PATH DIAGRAM

Alternate 1 knit and 1 purl stitch reversed in every course.

STEP 1: Alternating 1 knit and 1 purl
STEP 2: Alternating 1 purl and 1 knit

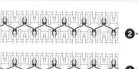

DOUBLE SEED STITCH
Used in place of plain stockinette for almost any type of knitwear.

LOOP DIAGRAM

FRONT

BACK

GATING SETTING
2 sets of needles in interlock gating.

NOTATION

YARN PATH DIAGRAM
Alternating 2 knit and 2 purl stitches in every 2 courses.

STEP 1 & 2: Alternating 2 knit and 2 purl
STEP 3 & 4 : Alternating 2 purl and 2 knit

 4→

 3←

2→

1←

CROSS TUCK

Combines a 1x1 rib base with a tuck in single jersey structure, creating a textured surface with a cross or diamond pattern.

Plain piqué technical back

Double piqué technical back

Lacoste technical back

IRREVERSIBLE

Not reversible; technical face and back are different due to the single jersey structure.

CURLING

Tends to curl toward the front at the ends and toward the back at the sides.

LADDERING

Can ladder from the last knitted course, but not the first knitted course.

GATING SETTING

1 set of needle bed

COMMON
APPLICATIONS

Sweaters

Polo shirts

Shoes

CROSS TUCK
VARIATION °1

PLAIN PIQUÉ

SINGLE PIQUÉ, CROSS-TUCK PIQUÉ, SINGLE CROSS TUCK

This fabric is durable and breathable, and is suitable for functional apparel.

LOOP DIAGRAM

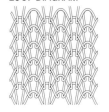

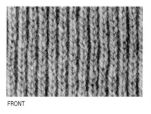

FRONT

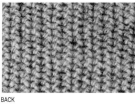

BACK

GATING SETTING

1 set of needle bed

NOTATION

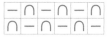

YARN PATH DIAGRAM

2-course repeat structure, alternating tuck and knit stitches; exchange stitching order in the following course.

❷→

STEP 2: Alternating 1 tuck and 1 knit

❶←

STEP 1: Alternating 1 knit and 1 tuck

CROSS TUCK
VARIATION °2

DOUBLE PIQUÉ

DOUBLE CROSS TUCK, DOUBLE LACOSTE

It is usually used to create unique coloration and subtle patterns.

LOOP DIAGRAM

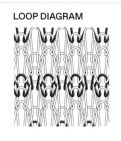

FRONT

BACK

GATING SETTING

1 set of needle bed

NOTATION

YARN PATH DIAGRAM

A repeating structure of 2 courses of single piqué.

STEP 1 & 2: Alternating 1 knit and 1 tuck
STEP 3 & 4 : Alternating 1 tuck and 1 knit

CROSS TUCK
VARIATION °3

LACOSTE

1 × 1 CROSS-OVER TUCK

A honeycomb-textured structure commonly used for polo shirts.

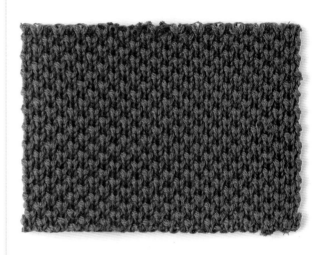

LOOP DIAGRAM

FRONT

BACK

GATING SETTING

1 set of needle bed

NOTATION

YARN PATH DIAGRAM

A repeat of 4 courses: A knit-stitched course followed by alternating knit and tuck stitches.

STEP 1 & 3: A course of knit
STEP 2: Alternating 1 tuck and 1 knit
STEP 4: Alternating 1 knit and 1 tuck

 4 →

 3 ←

 2 →

 1 ←

SKIP STITCH

Knitting skip loops in a course to create a unique texture or pattern with varied placement and length of float yarn.

LOW ELASTICITY

Elasticity is reduced due to skip stitches; float yarn has less stretch than loops.

LESS DURABLE

Less durable and less compact when more skip stitches are applied.

IRREVERSIBLE

Not reversible; float yarn is formed on one side or both sides.

LOOP DIAGRAM

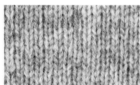

FRONT

BACK

GATING SETTING

1 set of needle bed

COMMON
APPLICATIONS

Details & patterns

RACKED STITCH

The racked stitch structure is a zigzag, herringbone-like pattern created by one lateral moving needle bed.

LAY FLAT
Does not curl due to balanced structure.

LOW ELASTICITY
Elasticity reduced due to tightened loops.

LOOP DIAGRAM

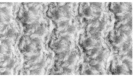

FRONT

BACK

GATING SETTING

2 sets of needle beds in rib gating. This structure is created by double bed machines.

KNITTING TIPS

① The size of the zigzag depends on the range of the racking action.

② Racking is more effective when one set of needles holds tuck loops.

COMMON APPLICATIONS

Tops

Details & patterns

MESH

An open, net-like knit created by arrangement of tuck and transfer stitches, resulting in different crochet, lace patterns.

LIGHTWEIGHT
Lighter weight due to lower density.

REVERSIBLE
Some can be reversible depending on the knit structure; holes can appear on one side or both sides.

LESS DURABLE
Structure is less compact and looser, making it less durable.

GATING SETTING
1 or 2 sets of needle beds, depends on the knit structure required.

COMMON
APPLICATIONS

Tops

Cardigans

Hats

Socks

Details & patterns

MESH
VARIATION °1

LACE (A-JOUR)

Creates open holes on a plain jersey fabric by transferring loops.

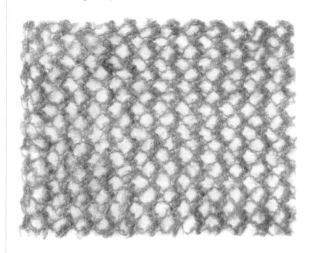

MESH
VARIATION °2

POINTELLE

A chevron-shaped lace with tiny holes utilizing transfer stitches on a rib knit.

MESH
VARIATION °3

RIB EYELET (OPENWORK EFFECT)
An openwork effect produced by transferring a
selected new loop from plain to rib or rib to plain.

MESH
VARIATION °4

IMITATION MESH (DROP STITCH)
There are many methods for making holes without
needle transfer on needle beds, and all these
methods called "imitation mesh."

INTARSIA

A knitting technique that creates blocks of color without carrying yarns across the back, allowing for complex pictorial designs.

*More colors can be shown in one course than with a jacquard.

LIGHTWEIGHT
Single layer structure makes it thinner than jacquard patterns

IRREVERSIBLE
Not reversible; knots are formed on the back side

CURLING
Tends to curl due to imbalanced structure on front and back

GATING SETTING
1 set of needle bed

KNITTING TIPS

① The beginning and end of each yarn color need to be hidden by making knots at the back.

② Each color is knitted from a separate yarn; the number of colors depends on the number of yarn carriers.

COMMON APPLICATIONS

 Sweaters

 Cardigans

 Dresses

 Socks

 Blankets

CABLE

A classic knit stitch is achieved by a wale or group of wales crossing over each other, creating variations of twisted rope or braid pattern.

THICKER & HEAVIER
Thick due to raised knitted texture.

IRREVERSIBLE
Not reversible; the cable only appears on one side.

GATING SETTING
2 sets of needle beds in rib gating.

STORY

Aran knitting is a style of knitting that originated in the Aran Islands off the west coast of Ireland, it is known for its intricate cable patterns. These patterns often carry symbolic meanings, such as the cable stitch, which represents a fisherman's ropes, embodying good luck and a prolific day at sea.

KNITTING TIPS

Yarn with a neat appearance tends to emphasize the 3D effect of the cable pattern.

COMMON
APPLICATIONS

Sweaters

Cardigans

Dresses

Gloves

Hats

SIMPLE CABLE

Baby cable

BABY CABLE
2-stitch cable crossed every 4th row

4-STITCH CABLE
4-stitch cable crossed every 6th row

MASTER CABLE
6-stitch cable crossed every 8th row

ECCENTRIC CABLE
Combination of different simple cables

CABLE
VARIATION °2

HORSESHOE CABLE

Also known as "butterfly cables", this is a stitch pattern resembling the shape of horseshoe. It is created by working a series of cable stitches that lean to the left and the right in a way that forms a U shape.

Double cable   Reversed double cable

CABLE
VARIATION °3

SLIP-CROSS CABLE

Created where some stitches are slipped (i.e., moved from the left needle to the right without being knitted) and then crossed either in front of or behind other stitches. This creates a twisted or braided effect.

PLAIT CABLE

This stitch creates a pattern that looks like a plaited (or braided) rope. It's typically made by crossing groups of stitches over each other in different directions in specific order.

PLAIT AND RIB

PLAIT AND ROPE

8-STRAND PLAIT AND SNAKE CABLE

OTHER CABLE VARIATIONS

HONEYCOMB

CABLE CHECK

ARAN DIAMOND
Diamond cable filled with moss stitch

CABLE KNOT RIB

OXO

CELTIC BRAID

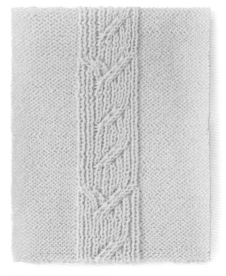

RIBBED ROPE CABLE

DIAMOND CABLE

JACQUARD

A complex, multicolored pattern knitting technique that creates patterns by missing or knitting stitches with different-colored yarns.

GATING SETTING

1 or 2 sets of needle beds depend on the type of jacquard.

Single jacquard: 1 set of needle beds.

Double jacquard: 2 sets of needle beds in rib gating.

Number of colors depends on number of yarn carriers

STORY

Fair Isle, named after an island in northern Scotland, is a traditional knitting technique producing intricate, multicolored patterns. Associated with signature Shetland designs, these patterns typically use a limited palette of around five colors. The style gained widespread acclaim in the early 20th century when Edward VIII, then Prince of Wales, was seen donning a Fair Isle sweater publicly.

COMMON
APPLICATIONS

Sweaters

Cardigans

Dresses

Socks

Blankets

SINGLE JACQUARD

Also known as float jacquard, it is a single-bed knitting technique for patterns with floated yarn on the back.

Floated yarn on the back

KNITTING TIPS

A tuck stitch can be used to shorten the length of float yarn for a larger jacquard pattern.

LOW ELASTICITY
Float yarns reduce the widthwise extensibility.

IRREVERSIBLE
Not reversible; the floats are visible on the back of single-jersey jacquards.

LOW DURABILITY
Tends to snag due to float yarns.

JACQUARD
VARIATION °2

DOUBLE JACQUARD
A rib jacquard that creates a complex pattern with two sets of needle beds. It has no visible floating yarn on the back side.

No floated yarn on the back

THICKER & HEAVIER
Thicker than single-jersey jacquard, as it is a double-faced fabric.

LOW ELASTICITY
Less elasticity than other knitted fabrics.

REVERSIBLE
Considered a reversible fabric with reversed color on each side.

DIFFERENT BACKING FOR DOUBLE JACQUARD

FACE

PLAIN BACKING
(Jacquard relief)

BIRDSEYE BACKING

HORIZONTALLY STRIPED BACKING

VERTICAL STRIPE BACKING

TWILL BACKING

REVERSIBLE JACQUARD
(Tubular jacquard)

DOUBLE FACE

A double-sided fabric with two pieces of fabric interlinked, often by a fine nylon yarn.

LOW ELASTICITY

Reduced elasticity due to the linking yarn.

STABLE STRUCTURE

Stable structure with linking yarn; able to give a clear and neat start.

LOOP DIAGRAM

Tubular structure-based, knitting with a fine yarn between front and back.

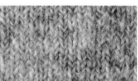

FRONT

BACK

GATING SETTING

2 sets of needles in rib or interlock gating, depends on the knit structure required.

KNITTING TIPS

Patterns can be created on only one side, with a solid-colored face.

COMMON APPLICATIONS

Outerwear

Cardigans

PLUSH

A plated fabric made from looped pile on the reverse side of some or all stitches.

Technical back

CURLING
Tends to curl toward the back at the ends and toward the front at the sides.

THICKER & HEAVIER
Thick due to the looped pile.

LOOP DIAGRAM

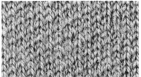

FRONT

BACK

GATING SETTING

2 sets of needles in rib or interlock gating, depends on the knit structure required.

KNITTING TIPS

A fur-like effect can be achieved with fluffy yarn.

COMMON APPLICATIONS

Sweaters

Cardigans

Dresses

Gloves

Hats

CHAPTER 5

KNITWEAR STYLES

Explore the diverse world of knitwear, where unique styles, intricate details, and distinctive finishes abound. Beyond fashion, discover the rich history and heritage behind various designs, making each piece not just stylish, but also storied and significant.

5.1

5.1

APPAREL

5.1.1
SWEATERS

First traced back to the mid-13th century, crafted by Muslim knitters for Spanish royalty, the sweater has evolved into a versatile fashion staple. Its styles range from traditional fishermen's garments to contemporary classics, showcasing its enduring appeal and functional versatility.

MEASUREMENTS OF A KNITTED APPAREL

■
FRONT

① *High point shoulder (HPS)
② Fashioning marks
③ Sleeve

④ Placket
⑤ Cuff
⑥ Bottom hem

■
BACK

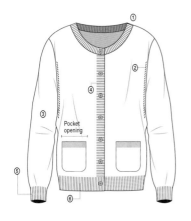

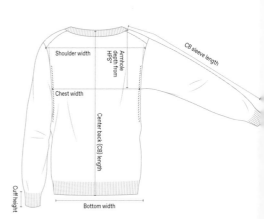

■
FRONT

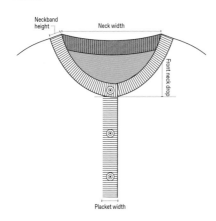

■
RAGLAN SLEEVE

CREW NECK SWEATER

V-NECK SWEATER

SCOOP NECK SWEATER

MOCK NECK SWEATER

TURTLENECK /
ROLLNECK SWEATER

FUNNEL NECK SWEATER

HENLEY SWEATER

SWEATER POLO

KNIT SHIRT

HALF ZIP SWEATER

HOODED SWEATER

SHAWL COLLAR SWEATER

COWL NECK SWEATER

TUNIC

SWEATER VEST

CUT-OUT SWEATER

CROPPED SWEATER

BATWING SWEATER

PATCHWORK SWEATER

GRANNY SQUARE SWEATER

CABLE SWEATER

MILITARY SWEATER

CRICKET SWEATER

Originating in England, the cricket sweater was worn over a player's shirt. Traditionally white, it features a V-neck, cable knit pattern, and often colored stripes or emblems representing the player's team or club.

MARINIERE SWEATER

ARAN SWEATER

Also known as a "fisherman's sweater", the Aran sweater often features signature complex, textured designs said to have symbolic meanings.

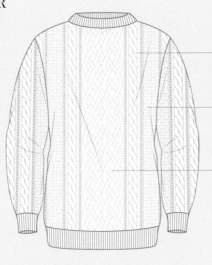

ROPE CABLE
Symbolizes a fisherman's ropes, it is associated with safety and good luck at sea.

MOSS STITCH
Symbolizes carrageen moss, which is a type of seaweed on the Irish coast. It suggests a respectable harvest.

TRELLIS
Often interpreted as a symbol of the stone-walled fields of the Aran Islands, it represents prosperity and success.

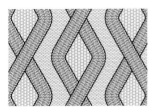

DIAMOND STITCH
Symbolizing the mesh of a fishing net, often represents wealth and success. When filled with moss stitch it is called "Aran diamond."

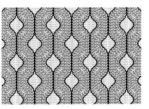

HONEYCOMB
Often interpreted as a symbol of the hard-working honey bee, it represents a good catch, hard work, and reward.

ZIG ZAG
Also known as the "marriage lines", representing the joys and challenges experienced in married life.

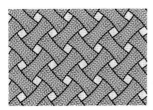

BASKET STITCH
Symbolizing the fisherman's basket and hopes for a plentiful catch.

TREE OF LIFE
Symbolizing a strong family unit, growth, and a strong lineage.

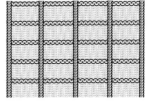

LADDER OF LIFE
Also known as "marriage lines", it represents the joys and challenges experienced in married life.

ARGYLE SWEATER

FAIR ISLE SWEATER

ICELANDIC SWEATER / LOPAPEYSA

NORWEGIAN SWEATER / LUSEKOFTE

GUERNSEY / GANSEY SWEATER

Originated from the British Isles and were traditionally worn by fishermen. It is traditionally knitted flat with heavily oiled wool and a short stand-up collar, so that it can be put on in a hurry either way round. It has distinctive pattern traditional to the fisherman's home port or village.

COWICHAN SWEATER

5.1.2
CARDIGANS & OUTERWEAR

A versatile, open-front knitwear piece, the cardigan is named after the 7th Earl of Cardigan. It's distinguished by its button or zipper front, and ranges from lightweight, draped styles to warm, chunky knits, perfect for layering in various climates.

THE CLASSIC TWIN SET

The twin set, a matching cardigan and pullover, was invented by knitwear designer Otto Weisz for Pringle of Scotland in the 1930s. By the 1950s, it became a common workwear for women in professions like teaching and secretarial work, and became chic when Hollywood stars such as Grace Kelly wore it on and off the screen.

Patti Page wearing a twin set with bullet bra, 1955.

ROUND NECK CARDIGAN

V-NECK CARDIGAN

DOUBLE-BREASTED CARDIGAN

SHAWL COLLAR CARDIGAN

ZIP-UP CARDIGAN

FUNNEL NECK CARDIGAN

ZIP-UP HOODIE

KNITTED BLAZER

OVERSHIRT

TIE-FRONT CARDIGAN

CROPPED CARDIGAN

BOLERO

WRAPPED CARDIGAN

COCOON CARDIGAN

PEPLUM CARDIGAN

BELTED CARDIGAN

BOMBER JACKET

CARDI COAT

DRAPED CARDIGAN

DUSTER

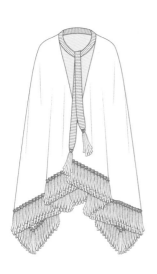

CAPE

PONCHO

5.1.3
DRESSES

BODYCON DRESS

SKATER DRESS

A-LINE DRESS

BELTED DRESS

OVERSIZED DRESS

OFF-SHOULDER DRESS

CAMI DRESS

CARDIGAN DRESS

KAFTAN

WRAPPED DRESS

CUT-OUT DRESS

POLO COLLAR DRESS

5.1.4
BOTTOMS

PENCIL SKIRT

PEPLUM SKIRT

PLEATED SKIRT

A-LINE SKIRT

FLARED SKIRT

JACQUARD SKIRT

CABLE SKIRT

TRACK PANTS

BELL BOTTOM PANTS

WIDE LEG PANTS

SKATER SKIRT

MICRO SHORTS

RUFFLE SKIRT

BIKER SHORTS

LEGGING

5.2 ACCESSORIES

5.2.1 HATS

BEANIE

FISHERMAN BEANIE / DOCKER CAP

SLOUCHY BEANIE

BOBBLE HAT

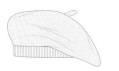

BERET

PUSSY HAT

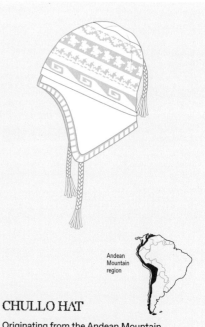

Andean Mountain region

CHULLO HAT

Originating from the Andean Mountain region of South America, the Chullo hat is characterized by earflaps and vibrant patterns, It's traditionally hand-knitted from alpaca or llama wool, providing warmth in high-altitude, cold climates.

CLOCHE

TURBAN

WELSH WIG	**TRAPPER**	**BALACLAVA**	**STOCKING CAP**

5.2.2
GLOVES

FINGERLESS GLOVES	**GLITTENS / CONVERTIBLE GLOVES**	**MITTENS**	**CABLE GLOVES**

FAIR ISLE GLOVES	**WRIST WARMERS**	**ARM WARMERS**	**MUFF / HAND WARMERS**

5.2.3
SCARVES & NECKWEAR

RIB SCARF

CABLE SCARF

SCOODIE

SNOOD

SKINNY SCARF

INFINITY SCARF

KNITTED COLLAR

FAROESE SHAWL

Originating from the Faroe Islands, the Faroese shawl is uniquely designed with a center panel and shoulder shaping to secure it on the wearer's shoulders without slipping off. Traditionally, it is knitted from wool and features intricate lace patterns.

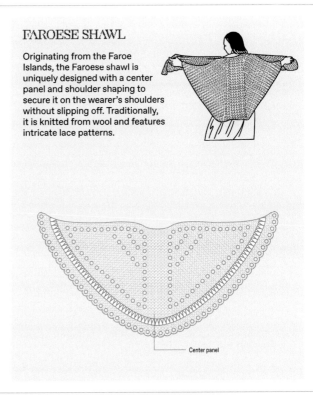

Center panel

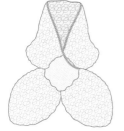

ASCOT SCARF

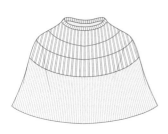

CAPLET

BIB

TRIANGLE SHAWL

5.3 STYLE DETAILS

5.3.1
NECKLINES &
COLLARS

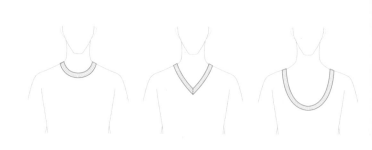

CREW NECK   V-NECK   SCOOP NECK

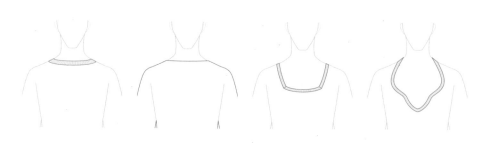

BOATNECK / BATEAU   SLASHED NECK   SQUARE NECK   SWEETHEART

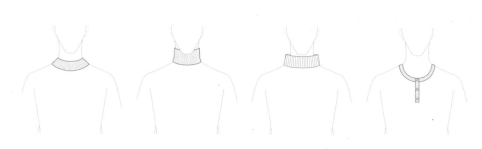

MOCK NECK   TURTLENECK /   FUNNEL NECK   HENLEY
                 ROLLNECK

STRAPLESS   ASYMMETRICAL NECK   ONE SHOULDER   OFF SHOULDER

CUT-OUT   SURPLICE NECK   NOTCHED NECK   KEYHOLE

QUEEN ANNE   HALTER NECK   RUFFLE EDGE   MANDARIN COLLAR

TIPPED

STRIPED

COWL NECK

JOHNNY COLLAR

POLO COLLAR

ZIP-UP FUNNEL

PETER PAN COLLAR

SAILOR COLLAR

PUSSYBOW

SHAWL COLLAR (PULLOVER)

SHAWL COLLAR (JACKET)

ASYMMETRICAL FOLD OVER

5.3.2
NECKLINE FINISHING

RIB
Single layer rib trim.
1x1 or 2x2 rib are commonly used.

DOUBLE RIB
Double layer rib trim, folded at edge.

RIB WITH TUBULAR
Single rib trim with tubular finish.

ROLL EDGE
Collar knitted with single jersey and
a natural roll edge.

TUBULAR
A fine trim option, single jersey in
double layer.

SCALLOP
Created by varied combination of
needle transfer and/or tuck stitch.

MITERED
V-neck hand-sewn to form a mitre
at center.

WRAP FINISH
Edges of the neckline overlapped
at center.

SELF START FULL FASHIONED
Knit to shape without additional trim.

LINKS - CREW NECK

LINKS - V-NECK

5.3.3
SLEEVES &
SHOULDERS

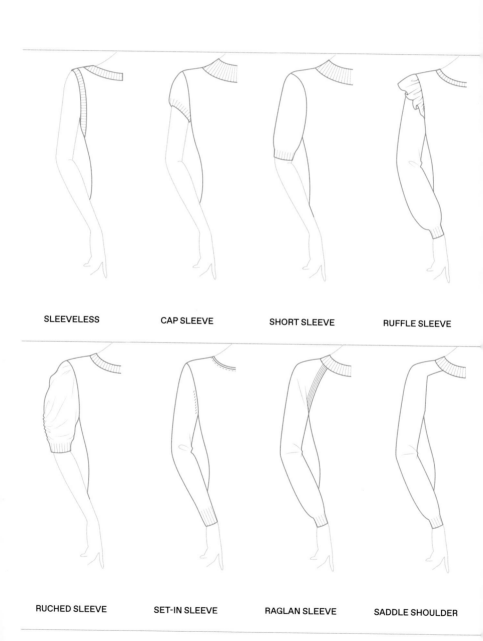

SLEEVELESS · CAP SLEEVE · SHORT SLEEVE · RUFFLE SLEEVE

RUCHED SLEEVE · SET-IN SLEEVE · RAGLAN SLEEVE · SADDLE SHOULDER

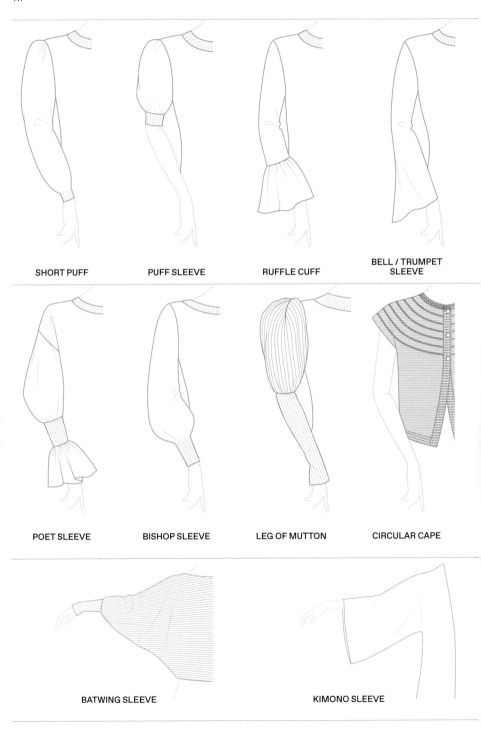

SHORT PUFF

PUFF SLEEVE

RUFFLE CUFF

BELL / TRUMPET SLEEVE

POET SLEEVE

BISHOP SLEEVE

LEG OF MUTTON

CIRCULAR CAPE

BATWING SLEEVE

KIMONO SLEEVE

5.3.4
FRONT OPENINGS

Remember: men's and women's garments open on different sides. Men's buttons and zipper pullers are typically found on the right, while women's are on the left.

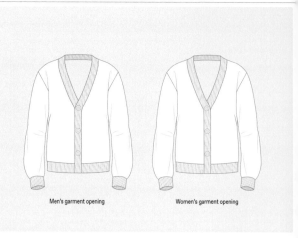

Men's garment opening   Women's garment opening

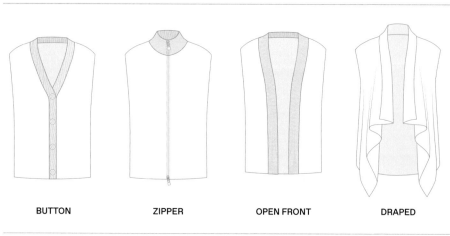

BUTTON   ZIPPER   OPEN FRONT   DRAPED

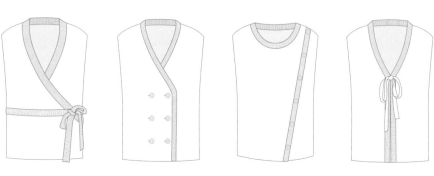

WRAP   DOUBLE-BREASTED   ASYMMETRICAL   TIE-FRONT

5.3.5
PLACKET
FINISHING

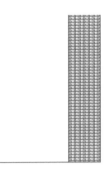

DOUBLE JERSEY
A stable structure often used single layer on button placket or open front.

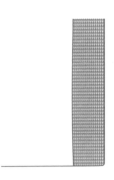

TUBULAR
Single jersey in double layer, slightly puffy effect

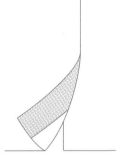

HALF MILANO
Applied on the edge for self-start effect.

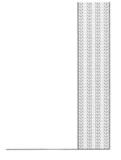

RIB
Often applied on open front styles in single layer. Tubular finish.

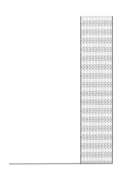

HORIZONTAL RIB
Can be applied on placket in both single and double layer.

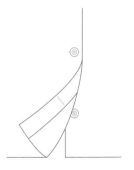

SELF FABRIC
Placket can be made folded or with strapping on the back.

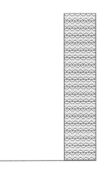

LINKS
A unqiue horizontal texture, often seen on whole garment.

DOUBLE KNIT SELF START
Clean sharp edge.

5.3.6
EDGE FINISHING

A range of stitches, structures, and color combinations allow for diverse edge finishes, applicable to bottom hems, cuffs, and pocket edges, enhancing garment aesthetics and functionality.

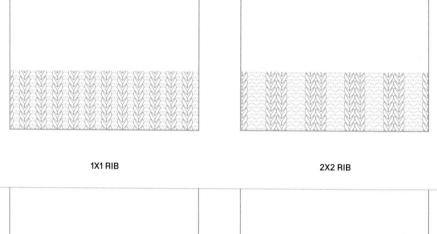

1X1 RIB

2X2 RIB

TIPPED RIB

STRIPED RIB

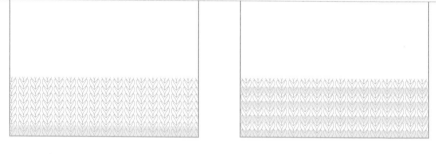

SINGLE JERSEY ROLLED EDGE

SCALLOP EDGE

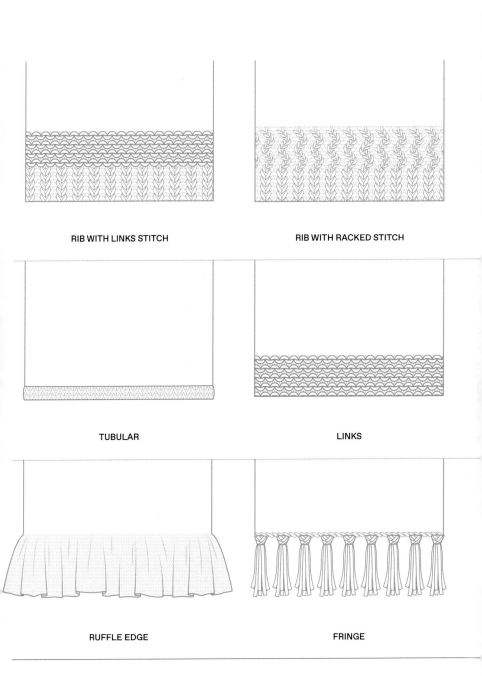

RIB WITH LINKS STITCH

RIB WITH RACKED STITCH

TUBULAR

LINKS

RUFFLE EDGE

FRINGE

CHAPTER 6

DYEING, PRINTING & EMBELLISHMENTS

Mastering dyeing, printing, and embellishments is essential for the visual appeal of knitwear. This in-depth knowledge elevates designs and ensures precise results, making these techniques crucial for achieving the desired impact in knitted creations.

6.1

DYEING METHODS

Dyeing can be done at any stage of production – fiber, yarn, fabric, or a whe
garment – to achieve the desired effect. For knitwear, fiber dyeing and yar
dyeing are more commonly used than garment dyeing.

6.1.1
FIBER
DYEING

This is done before a fiber is spun into yarn for a softer
hand feel, can be made into solid or heather effect.

■ STOCK DYEING

PROCESS
Bath dyeing loose fiber with
circulating dye liquor at
elevated temperatures.

RESULT
Solid-colored yarn

■ TOP DYEING

PROCESS
Winding fibers on perforated
spools at elevated temperatures.
The dyed top is then blended
with the other colored tops.

RESULT
Solid-colored yarn

Melange yarn

■ DOPE DYEING /
SOLUTION PIGMENTING

PROCESS
Dyes are added to the
spinning solution before the
fibers are extruded through
the spinnerets.

RESULT
Filament solid-colored yarn

6.1.2
YARN DYEING

This is done after the fiber has been spun into yarn. The color is usually richer and deeper. This method can also be used for making mixed-color yarn.

■
SKEIN (HANK) DYEING

PROCESS
Draping yarns over rungs in a dye bath.

RESULT
Soft, lofty yarns

■
PACKAGE (CONE) DYEING

PROCESS
Cones of yarn are stacked on rods, and dye is forced through the yarn under pressure.

*Commonly used on fine-yarn-count yarns and small size slots.

■
SPACE DYEING

PROCESS
Dipping or spotting colorants throughout the yarn.

RESULT
Multicolored yarns

6.1.3
GARMENT DYEING

This technique is also called piece dyeing, and is used in the manufacturing of fabric or knitwear. Allowances must be made for shrinkage.

■
UNION DYEING

PROCESS
Dyeing garments or fabrics to achieve a uniform color.

RESULT
Solid

■
CROSS DYEING

PROCESS
Using a single dye bath to dye fabrics made from fibers with different affinities for dye.

RESULT
Heather-like pattern / tweeded / striped effect

■
DIP (TIP) DYEING

PROCESS
Submerging part of a garment or fabric into a dye bath.

RESULT
Gradient

■
TIE DYEING

PROCESS
Binding a garment or fabric with string before dyeing.

RESULT
Unique pattern

6.2 COLOR APPROVAL

Color approval is a crucial step to ensure the accurate representation and consistency of color and shade across production lots. It involves examination under consistent light sources and across different material types to maintain color fidelity, thereby achieving uniformity in the final products.

6.2.1 LAB DIP

Lap dip is a laboratory dyeing process used to formulate a dye tailored for distinct materials, ensuring fabric color accuracy. It involves creating swatches or dyeing yarn in various shades to emulate a specific color. These lap dips are compared to the desired color standard under consistent lighting, serving as a visual reference for color matching throughout the production process.

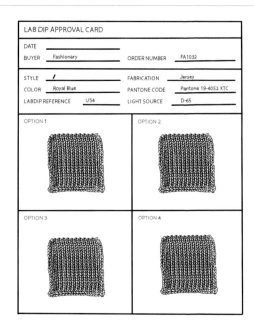

LAB DIP APPROVAL CARD

DATE

BUYER   Fashionary   ORDER NUMBER   FA 1032

STYLE   /   FABRICATION   Jersey

COLOR   Royal Blue   PANTONE CODE   Pantone 19-4052 XTC

LABDIP REFERENCE   U54   LIGHT SOURCE   D-65

OPTION 1   OPTION 2

OPTION 3   OPTION 4

6.2.2 DYE LOTS

Each batch of dyes in textile production receives a unique dye lot number. The purpose of this assignment is to monitor variations and aim for maximum consistency across different production runs. However, achieving a 100% match between diverse dye lots is impossible, due to variations in factors like production quantity, fiber construction, dye concentration, and temperature.

6.2.3
LIGHTBOX

A lightbox is crucial for color approval as colors can appear different under various lighting due to the material structure and dyestuffs used. The lightbox ensures consistency by providing a standard, reproducible illumination for color review. It can be adjusted to mimic different lighting conditions, enhancing color evaluation accuracy.

COMMONLY USED SETTINGS IN APPAREL PRODUCTION:
1. D65 (daylight)
2. TL84 (store light)
3. UV (to detect optical brighteners)

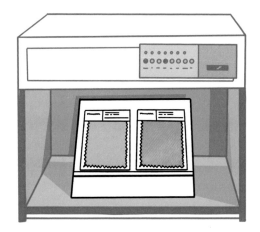

TIPS The aging of light tubes in lightboxes can result in color discrepancies. Consult your lightbox supplier for the recommended replacement interval for the tubes.

THE CRITERIA
FOR GOOD DYEING

1. ACCURATE SHADING
Correct luminosity, lightness or darkness.

2. EVEN COLOR
Same hue, shade, and chroma.

3. EASY APPLICATION
Technically viable, efficient and effective application.

4. COST AND ENVIRONMENTAL IMPACT
Low cost, less water use, and less damaging to the environment.

5. COLORFASTNESS
Colorfastness refers to a material's ability to retain color when exposed to conditions such as sunlight, laundering, perspiration, and crocking. Fastness is graded from 1 (lowest) to 5 (highest), with a grade of ≥3 generally accepted.

6.3 TYPES OF DYE

DYE CLASS	ACID (ANIONIC)	ACID MILLING	AZOIC *Prohibited in Europe	BASIC (CATIONIC)	DIRECT	DISPERSE
GENERAL DESCRIPTION	■ Water-soluble ■ Complete color range ■ Easy application	■ Water-soluble ■ Duller than acid dyes ■ Complete color range ■ Easy application	■ Insoluble in water ■ Complicated application ■ Prohibited in EU market	■ Easy application for acrylic ■ Complete and brilliant color range ■ Poor fastness on cellulosic fibers	■ Simple application ■ Inexpensive ■ Complete color range ■ Colors duller than basic or acid dyes	■ Also known as acetate dye ■ Good shade range
USES	Wool, silk, protein fibers, nylon, Spandex	Wool, silk, protein fibers, nylon, Spandex	Cotton and cellulosics	Acrylics	Union dyes for cotton / wool blends, silk, nylon	Synthetics and cellulose fibers
FASTNESS						
LIGHT	★★★	★★★	★★★★	★ Natural fibers ★★★★ Acrylics	★★★★	★★★
WASHING	★	★★★★	★★★★	★ Natural fibers ★★★★ Acrylics	★	★★★
PERSPIRATION	★★★	★★★	★★★★	★ Natural fibers ★★★★ Acrylics	★★★	★★★★
CROCKING	★★★★★	★★★★	Depends on dyeing technique	★ Natural fibers ★★★★ Acrylics	★★★★	★★★★
DRY CLEANING	★★★★	★★★★	★★★★	★ Natural fibers ★★★★ Acrylics	★★★★	★★★★

METAL COMPLEX	MORDANT (CHROME)	PIGMENT	REACTIVE	SULFUR (SULPHUR)	VAT
■ Complicated application ■ Expensive ■ Shades are fairly bright but less bright than acid dyes	■ Complicated application ■ Good fastness on wool fibers ■ Dull but wide range of colors	■ No affinity for fibers ■ Complete shade range in bright colors	■ Very good fastness, brilliant shades ■ Higher cost than some other dyes	■ Complicated application ■ Inexpensive ■ Colors are not bright enough for many uses	■ Most expensive ■ Incomplete but adequate shade range ■ Best all-around fastness
Wool, silk, nylon	Wool, silk, nylon cellulose fibers	Cotton, wool, rayon, acetate, nylon, polyester	Cotton, wool, silk, nylon, acrylic, blends	Cotton, viscose, rayon, linen, blends	Cotton
★★★★	★★★★	★★★★	★★★★ ★★ Nylon	★★ Yellows and browns ★★★★ Darker colors	★★★★★
★★★	★★★★	★★★★	★★★★	★★★	★★★★
★★★★	★★★★	★★★★	★★★★	★★★★	★★★★
★★★★	★★★	★★★★ Light to medium ★ Dark	★★★★	★★★	★★★
★★★★	★★★	★★★★	★★★★	★★★★	★★★★

6.4

COMMON PRINTING METHODS

Patterns or designs can be printed onto fabric in one or more colors by using dyes in paste form (inks) or other mediums.

REACTIVE PRINTING

After pretreatment, a water-soluble ink is infused into a garment or fabric.
The ink can't be felt, as it fuses with the fabric.

PROCESS

The ink is placed on a screen and each color is applied one by one. Heat and steam fix and dry each color. Finally, the fabric is washed to remove the excess dye and pretreatment.

COMMON MATERIAL

Natural fiber

CHARACTERISTICS

- Soft hand feel
- Bright colors
- Great colorfastness
- Good breathability in the printed area
- Not suitable for dark-colored garments
- The print can be washed to soften the garment and make it more comfortable
- The fabric must be washed to remove excess dye and pretreatment

PIGMENT PRINTING

A quick printing method in which ink coats the top layer of the garment without chemical bonding.

PROCESS

Ink is applied to a garment through a screen. After the ink has dried, it is fixed using a heat press, curing oven, or hot mangle.

COMMON MATERIAL

Natural or synthetic

CHARACTERISTICS

- Wide range of colors
- The surface of the textile is coated with a binding agent
- Printed areas are often stiff
- Average wet and rubbing fastness
- Considerably more eco-friendly, as less water is wasted
- Economical (requires less machinery)

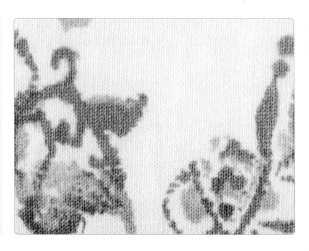

FLOCK PRINTING

An area of fabric is coated in adhesive, then short fibers are applied, creating a velvety surface.

PROCESS

An adhesive is applied through a stencil screen, then flocking powder is applied. Heat fixes the flocking to the surface.

*Flocking should be done in a controlled atmosphere for the best results.

CHARACTERISTICS

- Can be applied to any material
- Dyes and chemicals are not required
- Does not hold fine patterns well, print patterns should have a minimum width of 1.5mm
- Flocking is resistant to fading and cracking

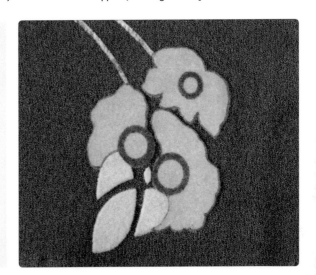

FOIL PRINTING

Adhesive and a sheet of metallic foil are applied to the fabric or garment surface, producing a shiny, mirrored look.

PROCESS

An adhesive is applied to the garment through a stencil screen. The garment is dried, then a sheet of metallic foil is heat-pressed onto the adhesive area. Once cool, the excess foil is removed, revealing the design.

COMMON MATERIAL

Natural or synthetic

CHARACTERISTICS

- The quality of the adhesive is important for durability
- The process creates shiny, mirror-like effects
- The foil area tends to tarnish or flake after many washes

DISCHARGE PRINTING

Discharge printing, also called extract printing, removes the dye on a garment or textile, leaving a light-colored area.

PROCESS
A discharge agent is applied through a stencil screen. The garment is then dried and heat-treated.

COMMON MATERIAL
Natural fiber

CHARACTERISTICS
- Creates sharp and fine patterns on dark fabric
- Good colorfastness
- The discharged area has a soft hand feel
- Costly due to the complex process
- Good for creating mottled patterns

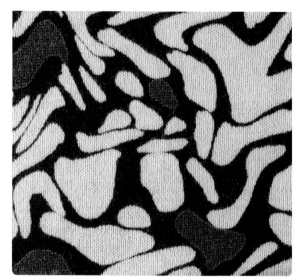

RESIST PRINTING

In resist printing, a substance – for instance wax, mud, paste or a chemical agent – is placed on a fabric or garment before it is dyed. When the substance is removed, it reveals a pattern or design.

PROCESS
The resist substance is applied through a stencil screen, then the garment or fabric is dyed. When the substance is washed off, the pattern remains.

COMMON MATERIAL
Natural or synthetic

CHARACTERISTICS
- Soft hand feel
- Good colorfastness
- Commonly used when the base color is difficult to discharge

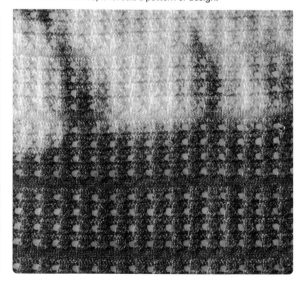

TRANSFER PRINTING

A design or pattern is printed on transfer paper, then transferred to the garment by heat and pressure. Transfer printing is quick and easy, and uses little water and few chemicals.

PROCESS
A design is printed on transfer paper, which is then heat-pressed to set the pattern on the garment.

COMMON MATERIAL
Polyester

CHARACTERISTICS
- Environmentally friendly; minimal use of water and chemicals
- Excellent sharpness of pattern
- Low colorfastness due to the dyeing ink
- Poor breathability on printed area
- Various types of transfer paper can be used
- Not suitable for printing on collars or seams

DIGITAL PRINTING

An expensive printing method with short development and lead time, digital printing is mainly used for high-grade knits. It is suitable for printing patterns with lots of color and shading.

PROCESS
A design is printed onto a garment by an inkjet printer.

PRINTING EQUIPMENT
Computer, inkjet printer

CHARACTERISTICS
- Excellent sharpness of design; prints fine lines and complicated images
- Fair colorfastness
- Wide range of colors available
- Quick sampling
- Usually few machines available in each factory
- Short development and lead time

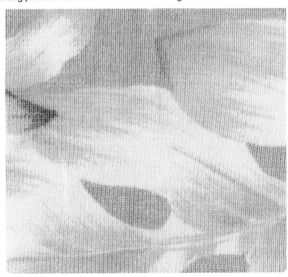

6.5

TYPES OF EMBELLISHMENTS

6.5.1
TYPES OF EMBROIDERY

FLAT EMBROIDERY

RAISED EMBROIDERY

YARN EMBROIDERY

RIBBON EMBROIDERY

159

CHAIN-STITCH EMBROIDERY

CROSS-STITCH EMBROIDERY

CHENILLE EMBROIDERY

APPLIQUE EMBROIDERY

6.5.2
TYPES OF BEADS,
SEQUINS & APPLIQUES

SEED BEADS

FLAT SEQUINS

BUGLE BEADS

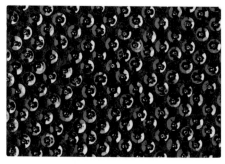

CUP SEQUINS

WOOD BEADS

PEARL BEADS

DISC SEQUINS

LACE APPLIQUE

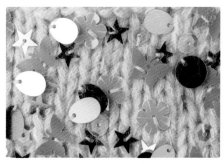

SHAPED SEQUINS

EMBROIDERY PATCHES

RHINESTONES

FEATHERS

CHAPTER 7

MAKING UP
OF KNITWEAR

The final stages of creating knitwear,
such as cutting, linking, laundering,
and adding finishing touches, greatly
influence the end product's look and
feel. Proper navigation through these
important stages ensures that the
finished item has a professional and
refined appearance.

7.1 PROCESSES

CUTTING

The knit-to-shape panel does not require cutting generally, whereas body length fabric and piece-length fabric produced by a circular knit machine does.

■

PRESSED BEFORE CUTTING
All pieces, including trimmings, have to be pressed and set to the stipulated measurement and shape before cutting.

■

SHRINK TREATED
Fabric made from natural fibers is likely to shrink, so it should be shrink treated.

■

CUTTING KNIT PANELS
The knit panel is knitted with cutting marks which could be pointelle or tuck stitches. It is also knitted with self-started trimmings, e.g., hemline, cuff. It is cut with scissors individually by hand according to the cutting marks.

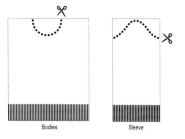

Bodies   Sleeve

OVERLOCKING (OVEREDGING)

The overlocking process stitches the seam, trims off the excess fabric, and binds the raw edges all at the same time.

■

WHERE TO OVERLOCK?
The raw edges of the cut fabric or fully fashioned panel should be overlocked to prevent them from unraveling or laddering.

Knitted fabric after cutting

Cut and sewn

Fully fashioned panels

Fully fashioned

■

OVERLOCKING CAN BE DONE IN TWO WAYS:

① In single-layer overlocking (commonly called overcasting), linking is carried out after overlocking.

② In double-layer overlocking (commonly called twin serging), two pieces of fabric are overlocked together. There can be linking after overlocking, or simply overlocking without linking.

■

THREE-THREAD OR FOUR-THREAD?
Three-thread is used for single-layer overlocking or double-layer overlocking.

Four-thread overlocking, in which one row of stitches is used as a safety thread, is typically a double-layer overlock without linking by the looper.

LINKING

Linking is a method of seaming/attaching knitted panels. It requires a skilled operator and is widely used in the fashion industry.

■
PRESERVING ELASTICITY
Linking fabrics together loop by loop does not impair the elasticity of the joined fabrics.

■
TYPES OF LINKING
Fabrics may be joined together along the knitted course, or a knitted course to a selvaged edge, or selvage to selvage, which is known as "point seaming."

	Selvage to selvage	Commonly used for joining seams
	Knit course to selvage	Commonly used for attaching pockets, trims
	Knit course to knit course	Commonly used for attaching ruffles, trims

■
LINKING MACHINE
The gauge of the linking machine has to match the gauge of the fabric.

HAND-STITCHING

Machines may not assemble some garments' parts due to limited capabilities or aesthetic considerations. Hand-stitching is required to finish the work.

■
AREAS THAT REQUIRE HAND-STITCHING
Neckbands, the point of a V-neckband, the bottom of a cardigan's placket, the pocket trim, and other pieces that require special attention.

■
RAVELING AND NEATENING
Raveling means unroving excess courses of knitwear. Neatening means fastening the yarn end or other loose threads with a latch needle or hand-sewing needle.

■
MATTRESS STITCHING
Mattress stitching joins the vertical edges of two knitted pieces with a smooth and almost invisible seam under alternate loops. The yarn is pulled firmly for a neat appearance.

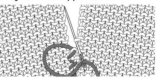

■
GRAFTING
Grafting is a way of joining sections horizontally. Both edges must have the same number of stitches, which are knitted together so the seam is smooth and elastic.

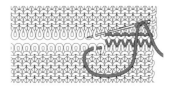

LAUNDERING

Laundering stabilizes a fabric's dimensions and produces a specific hand feel. The water quality, detergent, and laundering method all affect the outcome.

■ DECONTAMINATION

Uses detergents to wash and clean stains, oil, and rust spots. A tenacious stain must be removed with a spray gun or hand-washed before washing in a machine. The commonly used detergents are lye, washing powder, stain, and rust removing agents.

■ HAND FEEL

Hand feel is largely determined by detergent, water ratio, timing, rinsing (cleansing & softening) and drying temperature. Protein-based animal fibers will be weakened by alkaline and should be treated with pH-neutral or slightly acidic detergents.

■ SHRINKAGE

Washing helps relieve tension caused by winding and knitting, so as to stabilize the product.

TIPS

Laundering or pressing should be done prior to embellishment or buttonholing as the garment might shrink in water or under heat, that might lead to puckering or damage on the embellishments.

PRESSING

Pressing removes creases, folds, and wrinkles to produce a flat appearance, ideal shape, and correct measurements.

An iron pressing station with a vacuum ironing table is available to touch up the final product. Excess moisture will be removed to prevent distortion and clamminess.

■ HEAT OR MOISTURE?

Generally, the principles of pressing depend on the fabric's properties and its tolerance of heat and/or moisture.

■ NATURAL FIBERS

Moisture is important for natural fibers. They need to absorb it to become pliable.

MAN-MADE FIBERS

Heat is important for man-made fibers; they set more readily at a lower heat.

■ DEHUMIDIFICAION TABLE

A dehumidification table has an air outlet that dries the pieces as they are being pressed.

BUTTONHOLING & BUTTON SEWING

Lockstitched or chain-stitched buttonholes are commonly used on sweaters

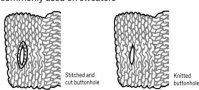

Stitched and
cut buttonhole

Knitted
buttonhole

■
COMMON BUTTON SIZES FOR SWEATERS

A sweater button usually falls into the range of 18 - 40 ligns. (1 lign = 1/40 inch)

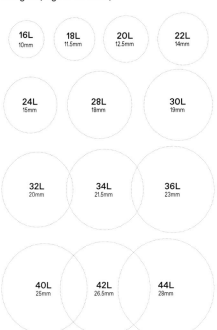

16L
10mm

18L
11.5mm

20L
12.5mm

22L
14mm

24L
15mm

28L
18mm

30L
19mm

32L
20mm

34L
21.5mm

36L
23mm

40L
25mm

42L
26.5mm

44L
28mm

LABELING

A main label, size label, and care label must be attached to knitwear for the consumer's reference. Care labels should include fiber content, with the percentage of each fiber by weight listed in descending order.

■
TYPES OF LABEL

FASHIONARY

Main label

Size label

75% COTTON
20% POLYAMIDE
5% ELASTANE

SENSITIVE WASH AT 30°C
DO NOT BLEACH
LOW IRON
DO NOT TUMBLE DRY
ANY SOLVENT EXCEPT
TRICHLOROETHYLENE

FASHIONARY.ORG

Care label

■
LABEL ATTACHMENT

BRIDGED
Stitching two sides

FLIED / HANGED
Stitching the top

HAND-STITCHED
Four corners

HAND-STITCHED
Top two corners

INSPECTION

There are three stages of inspection during which a faulty product may be mended or returned to control quality.

■
FABRIC
Fabric is inspected for defects and to ensure compliance with specifications. A fabric that can't be mended will be returned to the knitters to ravel and re-knit.

■
LAUNDRY
Before laundering, the product is inspected for workmanship flaws and damage. Stitches in the broken areas of a damaged product will shrink and fluff after washing.

■
PACKING
Before it proceeds to packing, the finished product is examined again. Final mending will be carried out if defects are found.

MENDING

Mending is the correction of faults by means of needlework, e.g. stitching. Skillful menders should be deployed at 3 points in production:

① FABRIC MENDING
   The initial fabric inspection

② LAUNDRY INSPECTION
   Interim inspection after assembly of the knitwear

③ PACKING INSPECTION
   Final inspection after finishing the product

PACKING & LOADING

Efficient packing and loading ensures optimal space utilization, reducing shipping costs and preserving garment integrity in transit.

■
PACKING
During packing, the folded product – which has been passed for shipment – is inserted into a polybag. Styles with buttons and additional embellishment must be packed with thicker tissue paper to avoid embossing.

■
LOADING
After inspection to ensure no needles have been left in the garment, the product is placed into the shipping carton. The color, size, and quantity are checked again in accordance with the buyer's order.

COMMON CORRUGATED CARTON BOX TYPES

3-ply corrugated carton / Single wall corrugated cartion

5-ply corrugated carton / Double wall corrugated cartion

7-ply corrugated carton / Triple wall corrugated cartion

7.2

QUALITY CHECK

Quality refers to a product's performance under actual usage conditions, specifically its ability to meet end-use requirements, both aesthetic and functional, beyond simply being free from defects.

QUALITY ASSURANCE (QA)
Product quality planning before production.

QUALITY CONTROL (QC)
Product quality inspection after production.

7.2.1
KNITWEAR TESTING ITEMS

Testing serves to scientifically inspect and evaluate product quality, ensuring the stability, durability, and safety of the product. Each brand sets its own standards according to their specific requirements and the region in which they operate.

PHYSICAL TEST
Evaluate the basic properties to ensure the material meets specified standards.
- Yarn count
- Stitch density
- Fabric weight

COMPOSITION
Identify the types and proportions of fibers used and ensure it aligns with labeling.
- Fiber analysis

SAFETY TEST
Checking for harmful substances that might cause irritations or other safety issues.
- Formaldehyde
- pH value
- Flammability
- Choking hazard test

PERFORMANCE TEST
Assess the product's durability under normal use.
- Pilling resistance
- Bursting strength
- Seam bursting
- Abrasion resistance
- Tensile strength
- Tear strength

APPEARANCE CHANGE
Analyze the aesthetic changes after washing or dry cleaning.
- Smoothness
- Color change
- Abrasion resistance
- Pilling
- Snagging
- Print durability

COLOR FASTNESS
Assess how well color of product withstands various conditions.
- Washing
- Dry cleaning
- Chlorine bleach
- Non-chlorine bleach
- Dry / wet crocking
- Light
- Water
- Perspiration

DIMENSIONAL STABILITY
Evaluate the product's shrinkage and ensure it maintains its size and shape after cleaning.
- Washing
- Dry cleaning

7.2.2
INSPECTION CHECKLIST FOR FINISHED PRODUCTS

CLASSIFICATION OF DEFECTS

CRITICAL DEFECTS
Grave adverse effect on basic function and safety of product.

SAFETY	APPEARANCE	HAND FEEL & ODOR
Sharp object inspection ■ Broken needles ■ Pins ■ Staples	**Bias or spirality** ■ Spiral side seam ■ Uneven collar	**Harsh and stiff** ■ Rough yarn ■ Tight stitches ■ Improper washing
	Holes ■ Broken ply ■ Laddering ■ Shearing ■ Seam raveling	
	Incorrect placement ■ Mismatching stripes ■ Unbalanced pockets ■ Uneven bottom hemming	**Sleaziness** ■ Loose tension ■ Flimsy body structure
	Design detail fault ■ Wrong knitting pattern ■ Wrong color ■ Incorrect design, e.g. print, embroidery, needlework, etc	
	Workmanship flaw ■ Unfastening of hand-stitching ■ Unmatched linking or sewing thread color ■ Poor mending ■ Linking too tight or too loose	**Odor** ■ Excessive amount of spinning oil ■ Packing without thorough drying
	Trim flaws ■ Placket too long or too short ■ Incorrect trims, e.g. buttons, zippers, ribbons, etc ■ Insecure attachment of buttons, snaps, hooks, beadings, etc ■ Zipper not operating smoothly	
	Non-smooth surface ■ Uneven yarn ■ Uneven tension ■ Knot / pilling / snag ■ Lycra sticks out	
	Stain ■ Stain removal haloing ■ Pen mark ■ Oil spot ■ Yarn dust	
	Foreign substance adherence ■ Fluff ■ Dead bug	

MAJOR DEFECTS
Expected to affect the ability and primary purpose of product.

MINOR DEFECTS
Defects are not expected to impede consumers from good and practical use.

INCIDENTAL DEFECTS
Relatively unimportant and not noticeable enough to become a concern for consumers.

SIZE & WEIGHT	ACCESSORIES	PACKAGE
Reduced or enlarged size ■ Shrinkage ■ Improper tension	Wrong main label and washing label ■ Wrong design / Incorrect wording ■ Missing label ■ Misplaced position	Improper folding ■ Does not fit in polybag
Asymmetrical knitted parts ■ Deviation of knitting tension	Wrong hangtag ■ Wrong design / Incorrect wording ■ Missing hangtag ■ Misplaced position	Mark occurs on product ■ Folding without tissue paper ■ Overpacking
Incorrect neck opening ■ Too tight or too loose ■ Linking without elasticity	Wrong spare button or yarn ■ Wrong color or size ■ Missing spare button or yarn ■ Misplaced position	Wrong packing method ■ Wrong assortment of color and size ■ Discrepancies with packing list and invoice
Heavier or lighter in weight ■ Variation between yarn lots ■ Deviation of knitting tension	Shoulder tape problems ■ Misplaced position ■ Wrong color ■ Color bleeding	Problem with carton box ■ Wrong size ■ Incorrect information

7.2.3
COMMON FAULTS & SOLUTIONS

YARN FAULTS

Yarns and machines are the two main sources of structural knit defects.

KNITTING FAULTS

These faults commonly occur on V-bed flat machines.

BROKEN PLY / YARN

CAUSE
- Poor yarn quality
- Improper storage conditions
- Worn knitting needles
- High winding speed during knitting

SOLUTION
- Mend by hand during inspection
- Re-knit the panel

HARSHNESS AND STIFFNESS

CAUSE
- Stiff fibers
- Improper twisting during spinning

SOLUTION
- Back-wind before knitting

DAMPNESS

CAUSE
- Improper storage conditions
- Improper spinning (unlikely)

SOLUTION
- Store at proper temperature and humidity

UNEVEN THICKNESS

CAUSE
- Uneven fibers
- Improper spinning treatment

SOLUTION
- Replace defective yarn

COLOR DIFFERENCES BETWEEN BATCHES

CAUSE
- Yarn dye in different dye lots or chemicals
- Improper dyeing treatment

SOLUTION
- Contact the yarn supplier for replacement

DISCOLORATION

CAUSE
- Sunlight damage
- Very humid or very dry environment

SOLUTION
- Store at proper temperature and humidity

ABRASIONS OR BRITTLENESS

CAUSE
- Improper spinning process
- Dry yarn
- High speed of knitting
- Improper knitting tension

SOLUTION
- Back-wind before knitting
- Adjust the knitting machine

UNEXPECTED SLUBS

CAUSE
- Impurities in fiber before spinning

SOLUTION
- Re-knit the panel

IMPROPER SELECTION OF KNITTING GAUGE

CAUSE
- Improper knitting machine setting
- Improper yarn count

SOLUTION
- Re-knit with suitable yarn gauge and count

KNITTING TIPS

For the best results, spun yarn should be back-wound before creeling.

Yarns can be thoroughly lubricated by means of paraffin disc wax, and faults can be removed from the yarn during the back-winding process.

BUNCHING UP
Fabric gathers into a fold

CAUSE
- Loops do not knock over properly due to a broken needle
- Improper take-down weight
- Consecutive tucking due to uneven yarn

SOLUTION
- Replace the broken needle
- Check the take-down roller or yarn quality
- Re-knit the panel

BARRÉ
A light and dark course-wise stripe flaw in fabric

CAUSE
- Difference in luster, dye affinity (or uneven dyeing) in yarn
- Improper mixing of fibers or yarn spacing
- Mixing of yarn lots
- Uneven loop length
- Defective plating

SOLUTION
- Check the yarn quality before re-knitting
- Re-knit with the same yarn lot, uniform tension on all feeders, and proper loop length or plating setting

HORIZONTAL STREAKS
Crosswise lines in the fabric

CAUSE
- Uneven yarn tension
- Uneven stitch length due to broken needle or cam setting

SOLUTION
- Adjust the yarn feeder, making sure there is no obstruction on the yarn path
- Check the condition of the needles
- Knit with equal stitch cam setting
- Re-knit the panel

FABRIC FALL-OUT (YARN BREAKAGE)
Fabric casts off accidentally
CAUSE
- Excessive tension in yarn or fabric
- Incisive needle verge
- Large knot
- Defective needle
- Improper stitch cam setting
- Unsuitable yarn
- Yarn with insufficient wax

SOLUTION
- Adjust the yarn feeder or fabric take-down force
- Replace the needle verge
- Check the knot catcher or pull yarn ends to the selvage
- Replace the worn needle
- Knit with equal stitch cam setting
- Check the yarn quality
- Mend by hand if defect is minor
- Re-knit the panel

STREAKS OR VERTICAL STRIPES
Lengthwise marks
CAUSE
- Tight needle in trick
- Bent or broken needle verges
- Poor needle condition
SOLUTION
- Remove dirt from needle trick
- Replace needle or needle verges
- Mend by hand if defect is minor
- Re-knit the panel

DROP NEEDLES (LADDERING)
Collapse of the loop formation in a wale
CAUSE
- Tight needle in trick
- Bent or broken needle verges
- Poor needle condition
SOLUTION
- Remove dirt from needle trick
- Replace needle or needle verges
- Mend by hand if defect is minor
- Re-knit the panel

CRACKS OR HOLES
Splits or openings in fabric
CAUSE
- Yarn knots
- High speed of knitting machine
- Improper fabric take-down force
- Stitch too long or too short
- Yarn overfeed or underfeed
- Yarn path obstruction
- Malfunctions of other machine parts such as needles, sinkers or cams
- Weak or dry yarn
SOLUTION
- Check the knot-catcher or pull yarn ends to the selvage
- Adjust machine speed
- Adjust take-down roller setting to provide proper force
- Adjust knitting tension
- Adjust rate of yarn feed
- Remove obstruction (e.g. wax and fluff) from yarn path (eyelets, yarn guides and tension discs)
- Check and replace worn machine parts
- Check yarn quality
- Mend small holes by hand
- Re-knit the panel

TUCKS, DOUBLE STITCHES OR FISHEYES
Inadvertent tucks in the fabric
CAUSE
- Poor needle condition
- Thick knots in yarn
- Insufficient fabric take-down force
- Improper tension, unable to cast stitches off
SOLUTION
- Replace worn needle
- Check the knot-catcher or pull yarn ends to the selvage
- Adjust the fabric take-down force
- Apply suitable knitting tension
- Mend by hand if defect is minor
- Re-knit the panel

LOOSE CAST-ON
Tension of set-up course is not tight enough
CAUSE
- Loose tension of the set-up course
- The wire of the set-up comb is too thick
SOLUTION
- Re-knit with a tight cast-on course and use nylon as the draw thread

SNAGS

Yarn pulled course-wise in knitting

CAUSE

- Improper use of yarn (especially filament yarns)
- Incorrect selection of knit or float stitches
- Stitch is pulled accidentally

SOLUTION

- Use a coarser count or a higher twist of yarn, or lower crimp elasticity
- Apply tuck stitch
- Tie thrums with needle work rather than by hand knotting (for intarsia fabric)
- Mend or re-knit the panel

POOR SELVAGE

Rough and loose longitudinal edge in knitted panel

CAUSE

- Insufficient or uneven fabric take-down force
- Inappropriate yarn tension

SOLUTION

- Apply proper take-down setting
- Check yarn feeder, yarn carrier stop and tension spring
- Re-knit the panel

LOOSE STITCH

A row of longer, larger and looser loops on the fabric

CAUSE

- Displacement of stitch cam
- Obstruction in the yarn path

SOLUTION

- Adjust stitch cam for proper tension
- Remove obstruction from the yarn path
- Re-knit the panel

FLUFF (COLOR FLY)

A small amount of colored fiber has been spun into the yarn / knitted into the fabric

CAUSE

- Remaining natural remnants or fluff while spinning
- Fluff from machine

SOLUTION

- Remove fluff with tweezers
- Re-knit with clean yarn and a clean machine

SPOILS

Stains or blurry spots on fabric

CAUSE

- Dirt or rust in needle tricks
- Oily or dirty machine parts such as needle beds, yarn carrier sliding boxes or guide rails

SOLUTION

- Remove dirt from fabric before linking
- Re-knit with a clean machine

INCORRECT PATTERN

Pattern is enlarged, reduced or deformed, or is in wrong placement or color

CAUSE

- Incorrect pattern drawing
- Inaccurate calculation of knitting scheme
- Inaccurate needle selection
- Loose or tight stitch tension
- Wrong color

SOLUTION

- Re-knit with correct information or knitting scheme

INCORRECT SIZE OR WEIGHT

Off-size and overweight or lightening of fabric

CAUSE

- Loose or tight stitch tension
- Inaccurate calculation of knitting scheme
- Wrong yarn color or yarn count

SOLUTION

- Adjust knitting tension
- Re-knit with suitable yarn or correct knitting scheme

SLURGALLING

Tight loop length along a single course or between courses

CAUSE

- Fluctuation of stitch cam
- Tight yarn tension

SOLUTION

- Apply stable and equal stitch cam tension
- Remove obstruction from yarn path
- Re-knit the panel

DYEING FAULTS

Imperfections can arise during the dyeing process; these may be due to flaws in the yarn or fabric, faulty preparation of the product before dyeing, improper dyeing, or post-dyeing procedures.

SOLUTION FOR ALL DYEING FAULTS
- Check with the yarn supplier

BLEEDING
Color loss from a fabric can result in the discoloration or staining of another piece of fabric

CAUSE
- Contact with liquid

CROCKING
Discoloration or fading

CAUSE
- Contact with another fabric

OFF SHADE
Color mismatched to the standard or lab-dip

CAUSE
- Faulty dye formulation or application, or variation in the dye lot

SHADE BAR
A horizontal band of a different hue running across the fabric

CAUSE
- A change of yarn cone that varies in shade or tension

SHADING
Uneven colors in a fabric

CAUSE
- Unevenness of yarn, unlevelled shade between the surface and inner layer in cone dyeing, improper dyeing, or uneven tension in the fabric

STAINING
Contamination by a foreign substance

CAUSE
- Grease, oil or residue of auxiliaries to the fiber or fabric being dyed

STREAKING
Staining or uneven dyeing

CAUSE
- Folds in the fabric

COLOR PATCHES

CAUSE
- Unremoved stains before dyeing

LINKING THREAD COLOR DIFFERENCE

CAUSE
- Linking thread has not been color-matched before dyeing

MAKING UP FAULTS

LINKING FAULTS

CUTTING FAULTS
Defective fabric cut

CAUSE
- Unstable non-shrink fabric size
- Inconsistent pattern position
- Fabric was not checked before cutting
- Deviation of position on the paper pattern

SOLUTION
- Inspect before cutting
- Re-cut the fabric

SEWING AND OVERLOCKING FAULTS
Uneven seam allowance, uneven stitches or distorted overlocking stitches

CAUSE
- Incorrect thickness of sewing or overlocking thread
- Improper stitches
- Sewing fabric without pre-shrinkage or setting

SOLUTION
- Sew with proper thread and stitches
- Ensure the fabric is completely washed and pressed

UNEVEN ELASTICITY BETWEEN DIFFERENT GARMENT PARTS

CAUSE
- Improper linking yarn tension
- Improper linking yarn

SOLUTION
- Avoid using low-elastic yarn as linking yarn

HAND-STITCHING AND MENDING FAULTS
Untrimmed seam threads; trimming too loose or too tight; inferior mending; incorrect patching yarn

CAUSE
- The inside / reverse of the garment was not checked properly
- Carelessness

SOLUTION
- Improve quality control
- Redo the hand-stitching

BUTTONHOLING AND BUTTON SEWING FAULTS

CAUSE
- Mismatched buttonholing, ragged edges and crooked plackets
- Incorrect buttonhole size
- Wrong or defective button
- Improper button placement
- Insecure, missing, or incorrectly attached spare buttons

SOLUTION
- Redo the buttonhole

MISMATCHED PATTERNS OR STRIPES
At shoulder seam, side seam, underarm or pockets

CAUSE
- Mismatching pattern and seam

SOLUTION
- Check the knitted panels; re-knit if patterns or stripes are not matching
- Apply correct placement before linking

PUCKERING / SELVAGE NOT STRAIGHT / UNEVEN SEAM ALLOWANCE

CAUSE
- Uneven linking placement

SOLUTION
- Apply correct placement before linking, and link with matching stitches

WRONG LINKING YARN

CAUSE
- Color difference of linking thread (yarn)
- Incorrect yarn count of linking thread

SOLUTION
- Linking yarn should be the same color and thickness as the body fabric

UNEVEN, DISTORTED STITCHES

CAUSE
- Incorrect linking tension

SOLUTION
- Apply proper linking tension

LAUNDERING FAULTS

WASHING FAULTS

KNITTING COURSES ARE RAVELED

CAUSE
- Washing fabric without proper overlocking

SOLUTION
- Re-knit the fabric and overlock before washing

SUBSTANDARD FUZZING OR FELTED WASHED FABRIC

CAUSE
- Incorrect detergent or softener
- Overwashing
- Overdrying

SOLUTION
- Re-knit and re-wash with proper washing and drying treatments
- Adjust the amount of detergent or softener

TINT MARK

CAUSE
- Washing agents have not been well agitated

SOLUTION
- Re-knit and re-wash using well-mixed washing agents

SULLYING, UNEVEN COLOR OR COLOR FADING

CAUSE
- Multicolored fabrics
- Mixing apparels with different colors during washing, extracting or drying
- Color bleeding from accessories such as lace, embroidery or buttons
- Improper washing agents

SOLUTION
- Re-knit or re-wash with proper washing treatments
- Separate apparel by color before washing
- Ensure that there is no color bleeding from yarns or accessories before re-knitting

DAMAGED OR DEFORMED FABRIC

CAUSE
- Using improper washing or bleaching agents
- Overheating in dryer

SOLUTION
- Re-knit and re-wash
- Apply proper agents for specific material-made fabrics
- Dry at proper temperature

FLUFF ATTACHED TO FABRIC

CAUSE
- Fluff accumulates in tumble dryer

SOLUTION
- Use a clean dryer

PRESSING FAULTS

POOR SHAPE

CAUSE
- Improper pressing board

SOLUTION
- Use proper pressing board

GLARING SHINE MARKS, WRINKLES OR BURNS

CAUSE
- Overheated pressing

SOLUTION
- Re-knit and press using proper temperature

INCORRECT SIZE / ASYMMETRICAL FRONT AND BACK BODIES, LEFT AND RIGHT SLEEVES OR TROUSER LEGS / UNSTABLE DIMENSIONS

CAUSE
- Using too much force when pressing, which affects the fabric's shape
- Pressing without dehumidifying

SOLUTION
- Re-knit
- Dehumidify the garment, then press it

HEM OR CUFF CURLING

CAUSE
- Structural imbalance

SOLUTION
- Process laundering along with waste courses, and remove after laundering

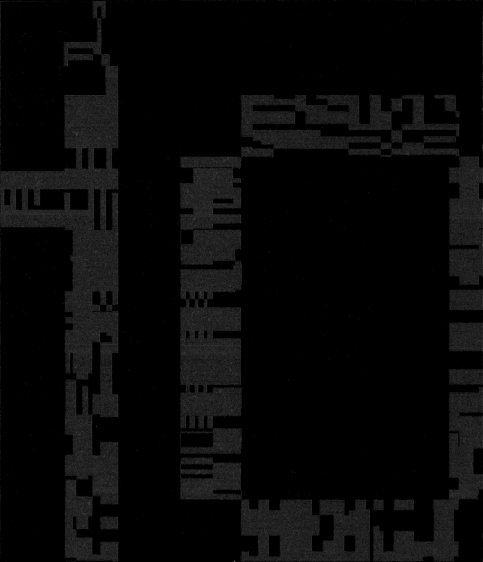

PATTERN

01

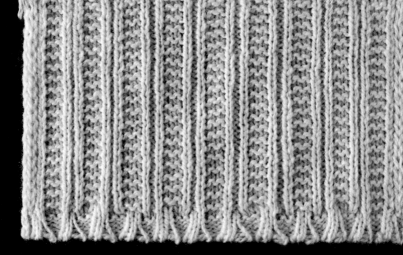

02

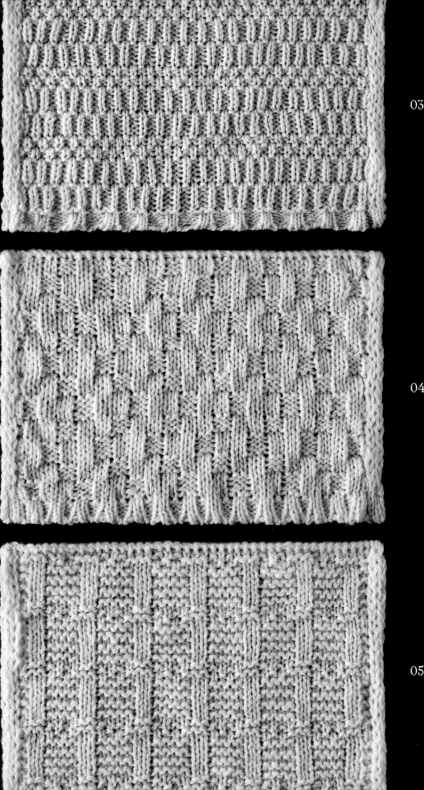

03

04

05

06

07

10

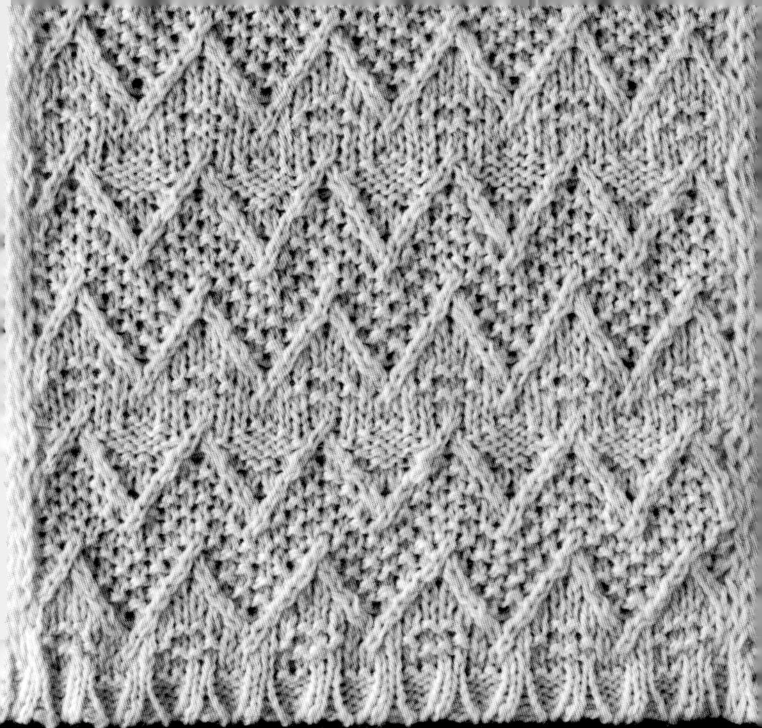

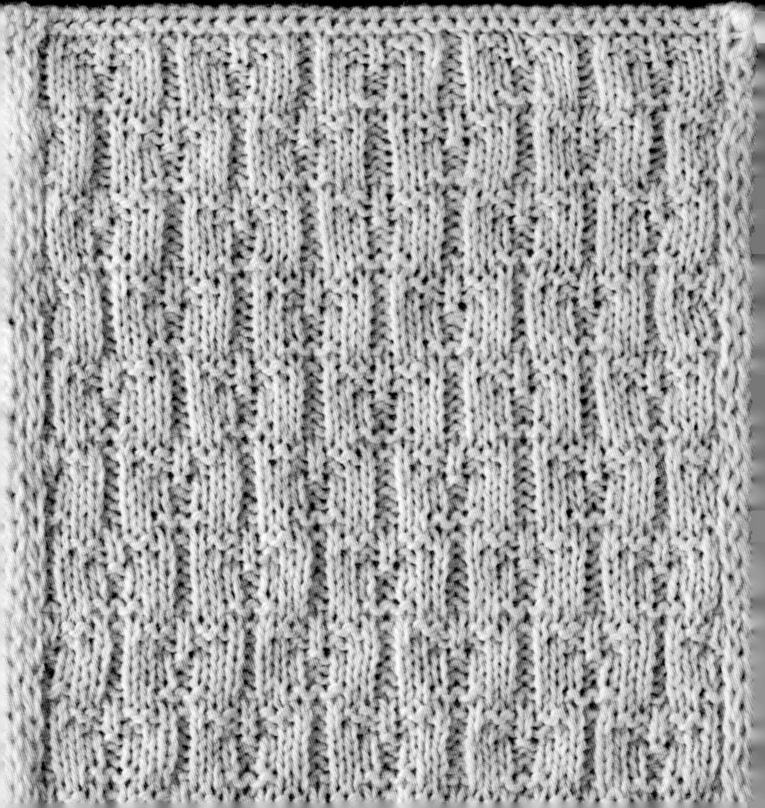

13

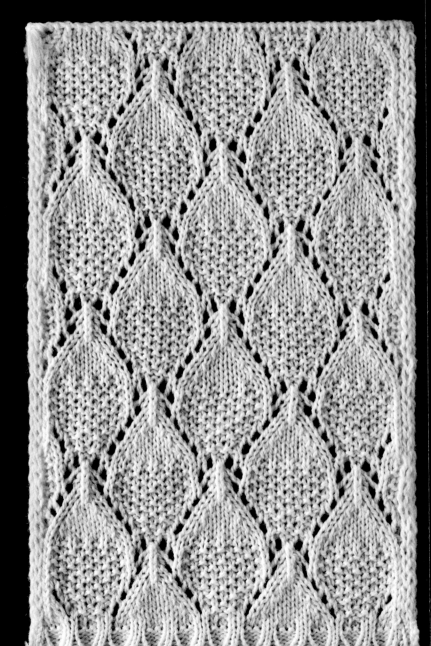

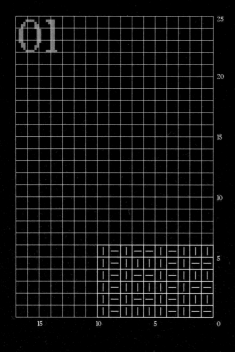

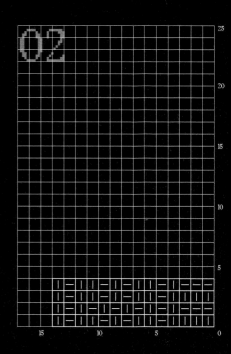

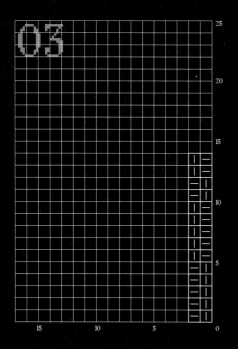

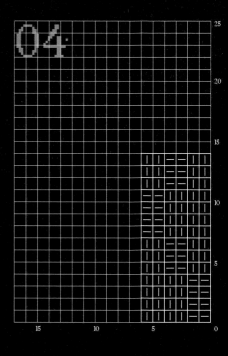

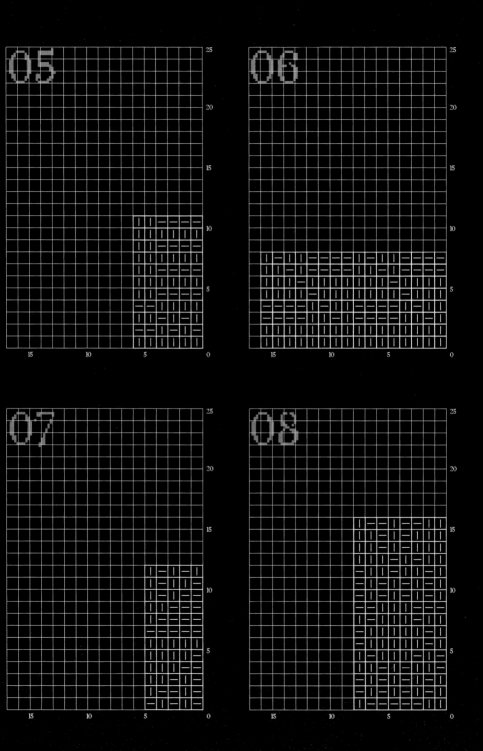

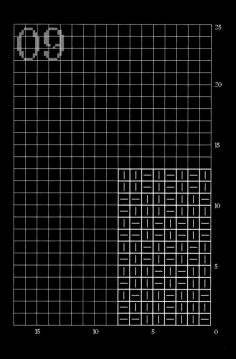

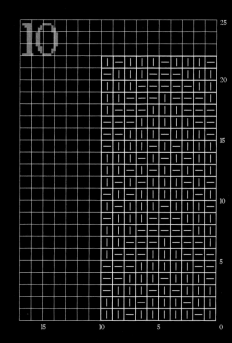

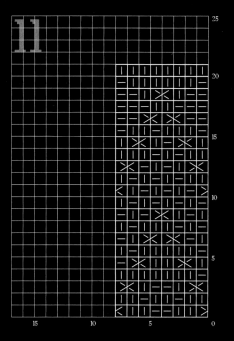

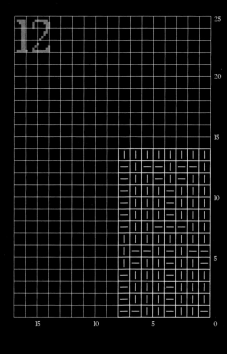

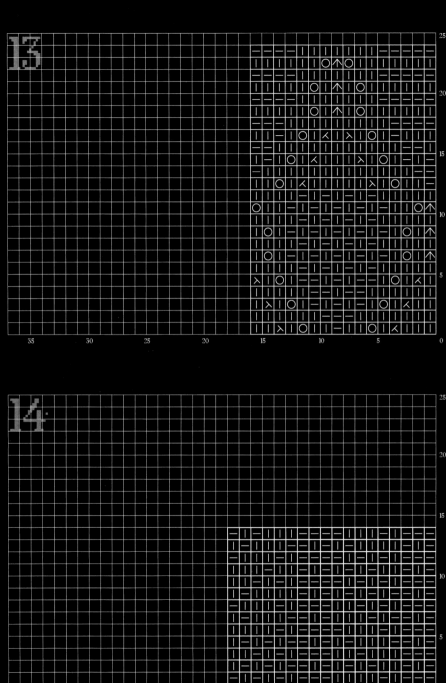

MESH

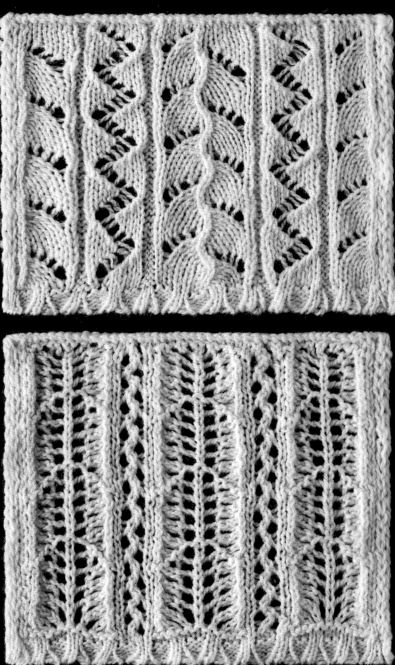

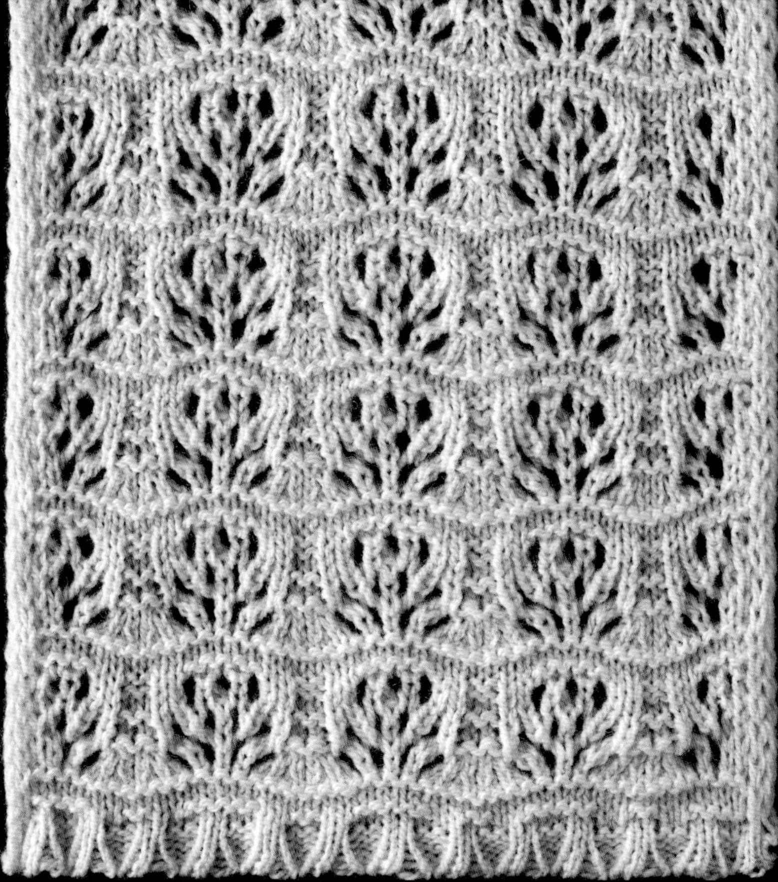
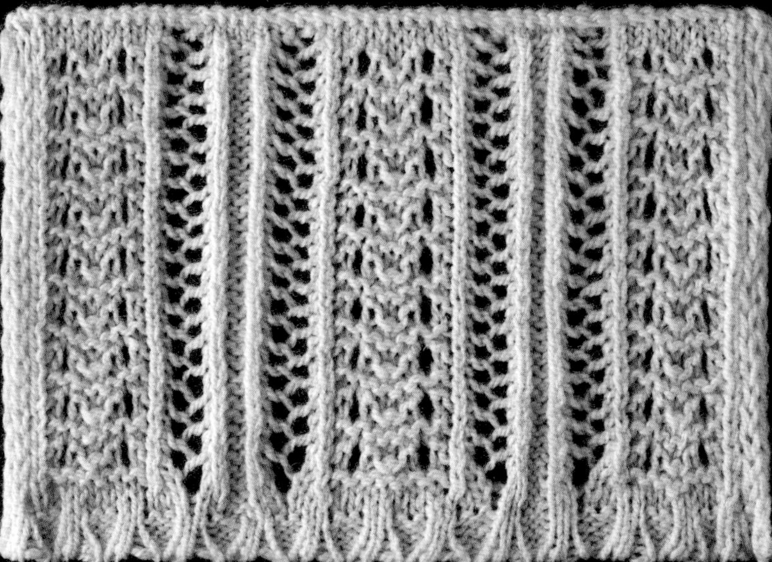

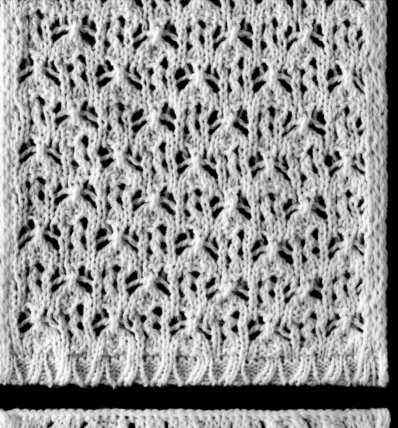

28

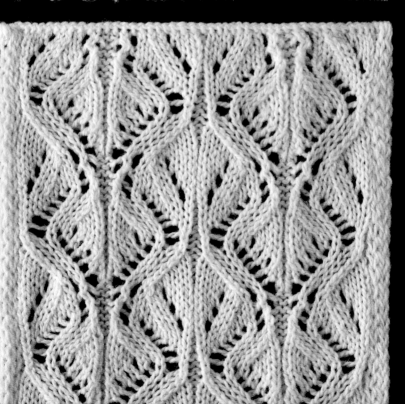

29

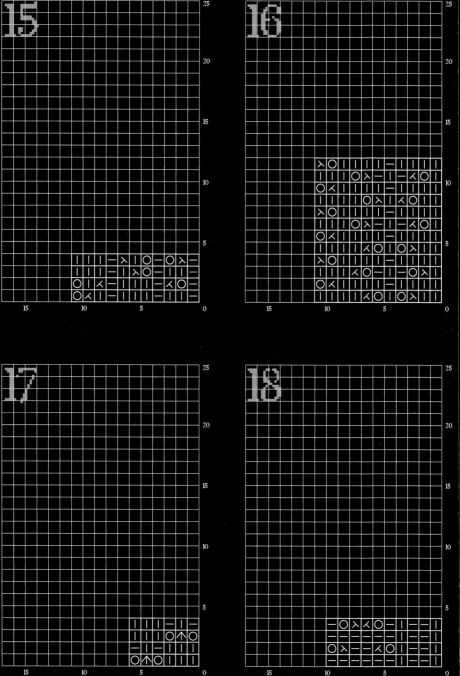

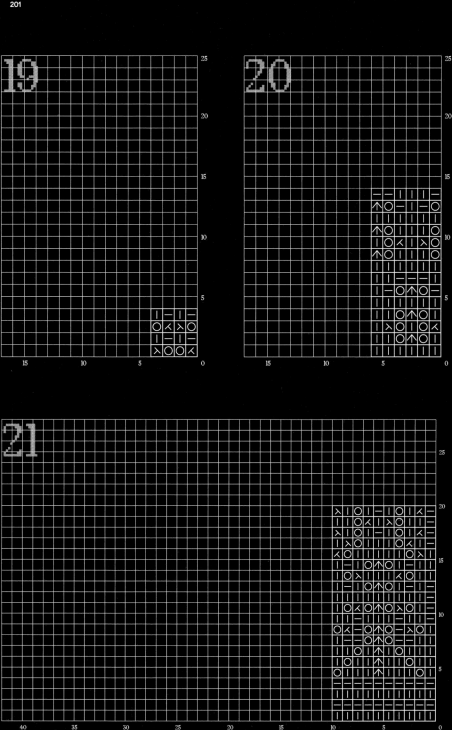

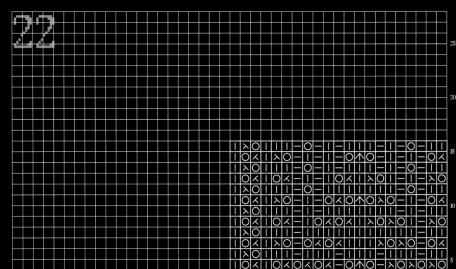

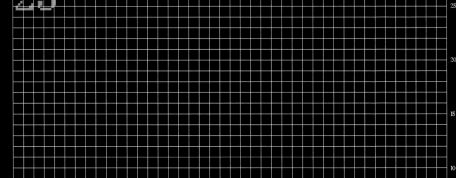

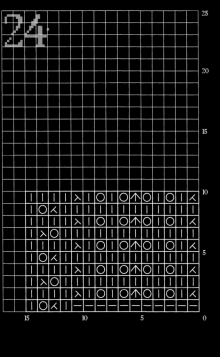

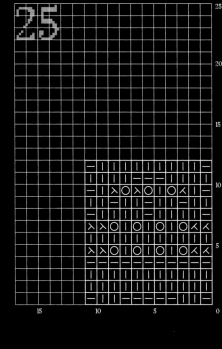

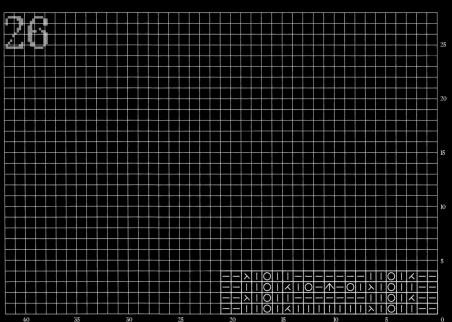

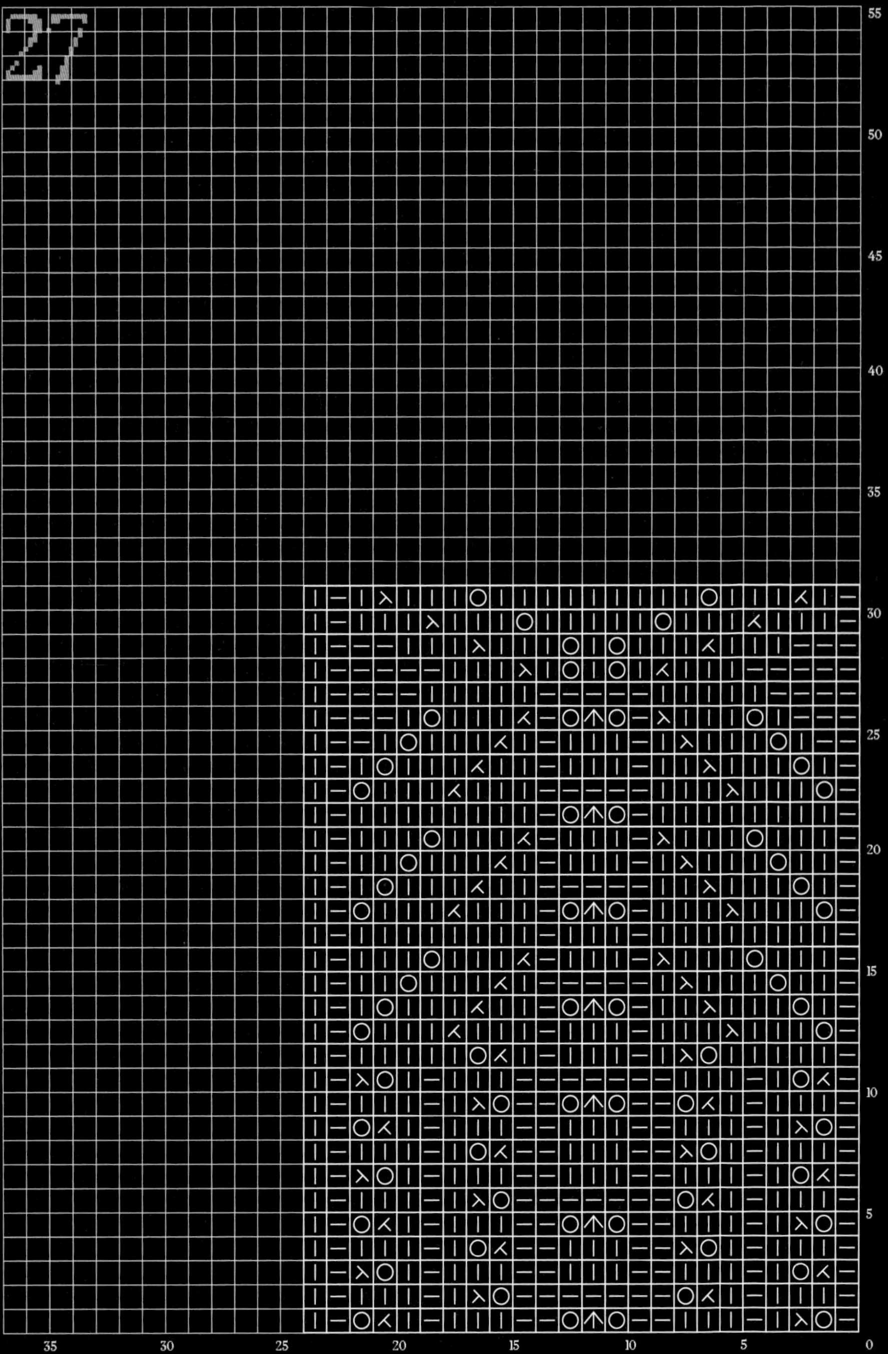
27

28

Chart 28 — vertical axis: 25, 20, 15, 10, 5; horizontal axis: 40, 35, 30, 25, 20, 15, 10, 5, 0

Chart 29 — vertical axis: 25, 20, 15, 10, 5; horizontal axis: 40, 35, 30, 25, 20, 15, 10, 5, 0

CABLE

30

31

32

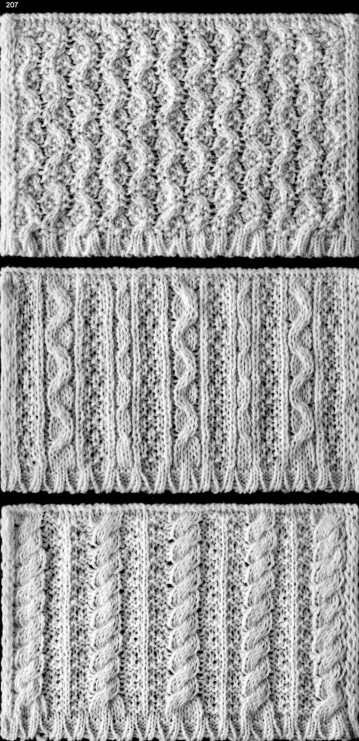

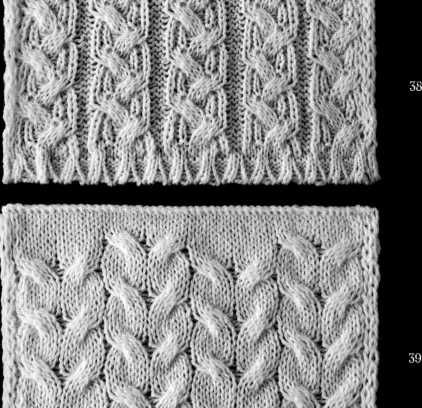

38

39

40

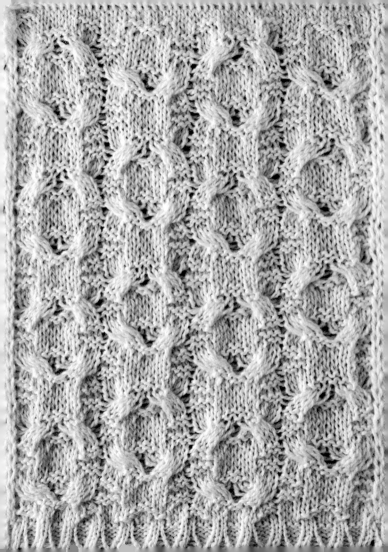

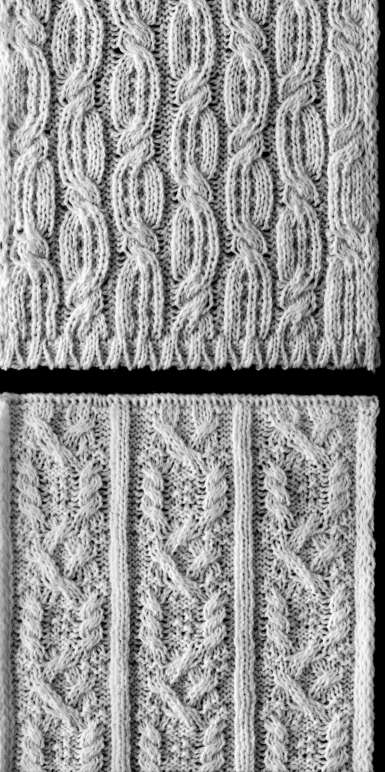

42

43

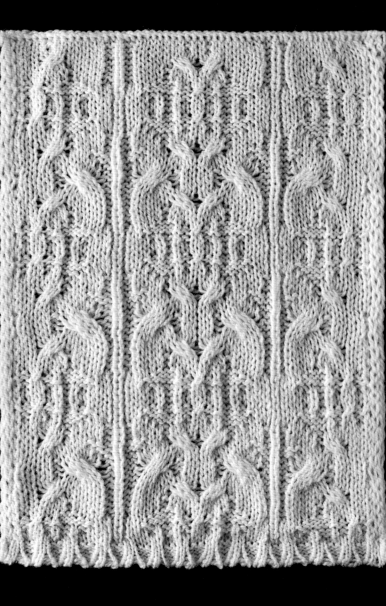

46

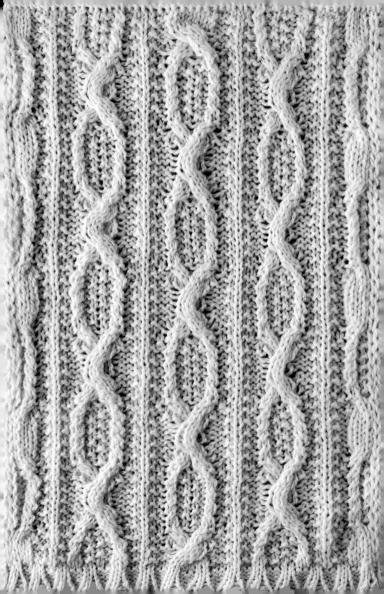

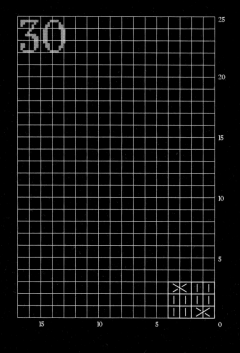

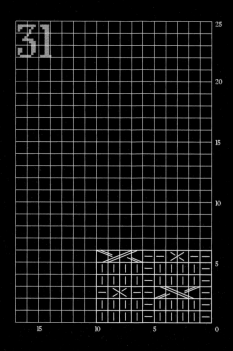

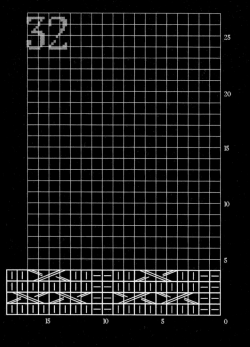

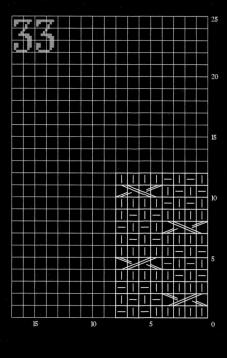

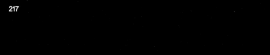

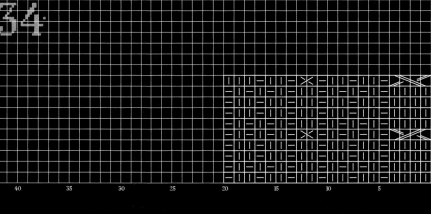

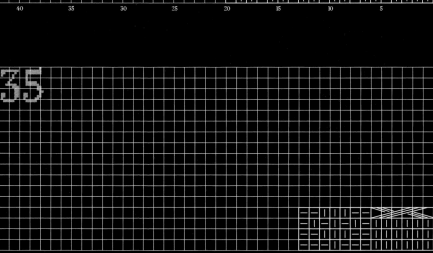

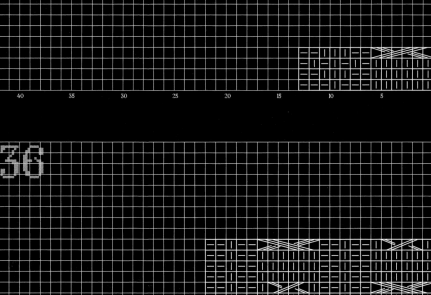

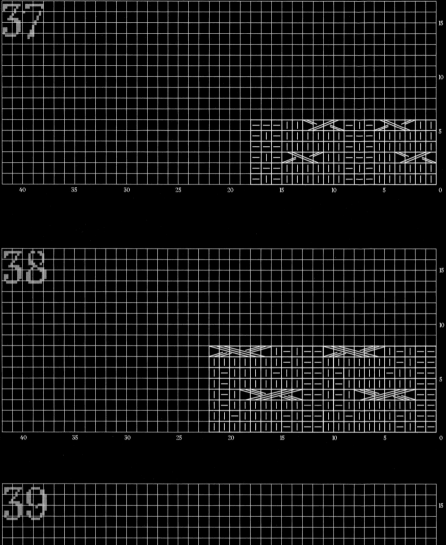

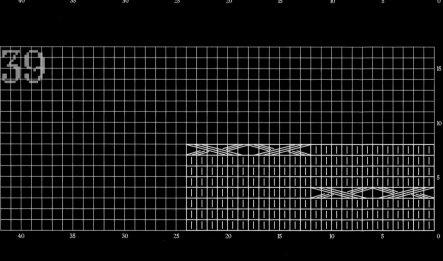

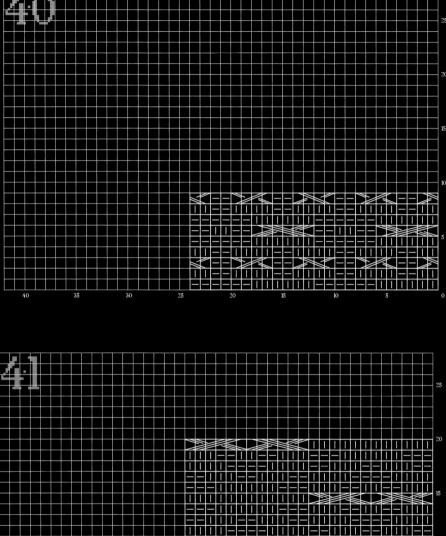

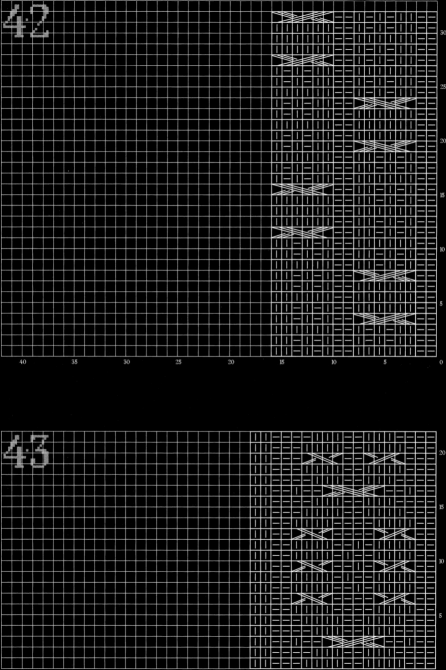

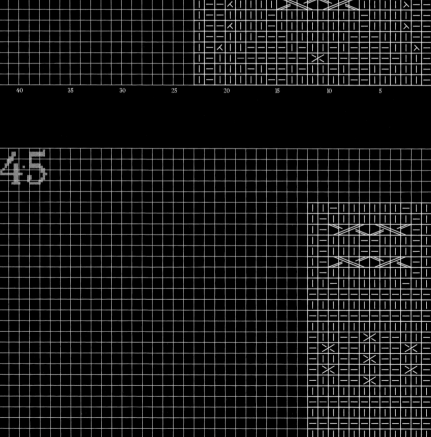

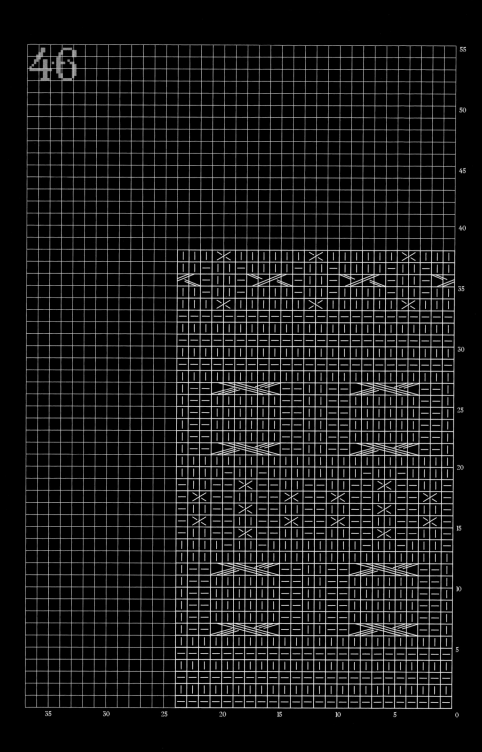

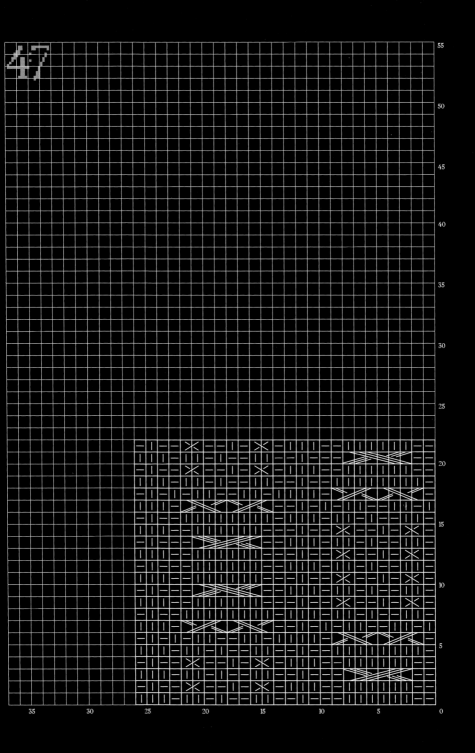

48

49

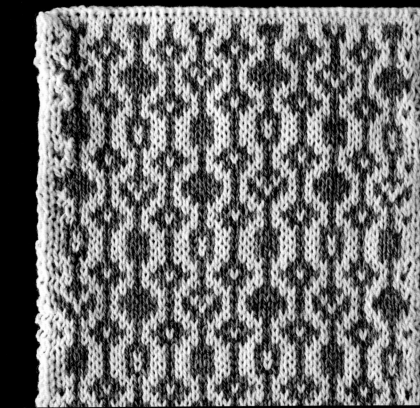

53

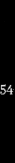

54

57   58

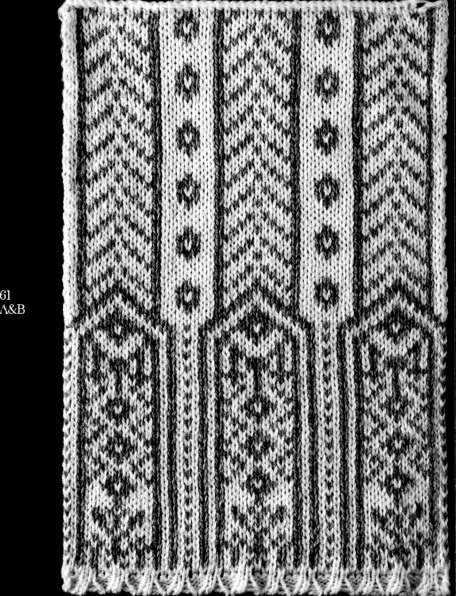

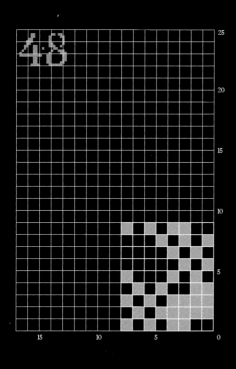

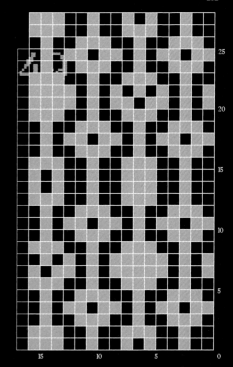

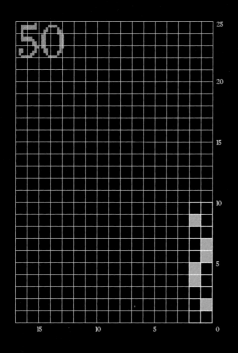

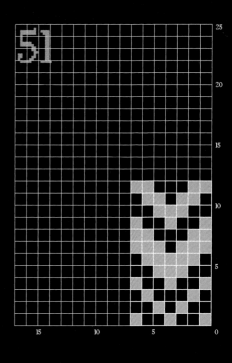

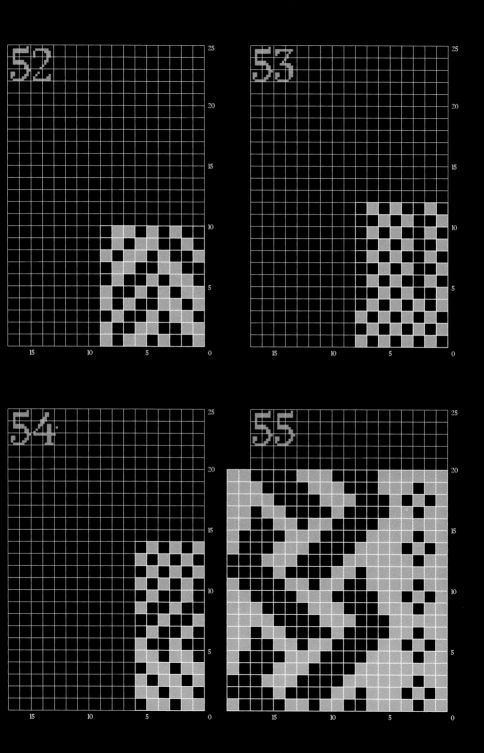

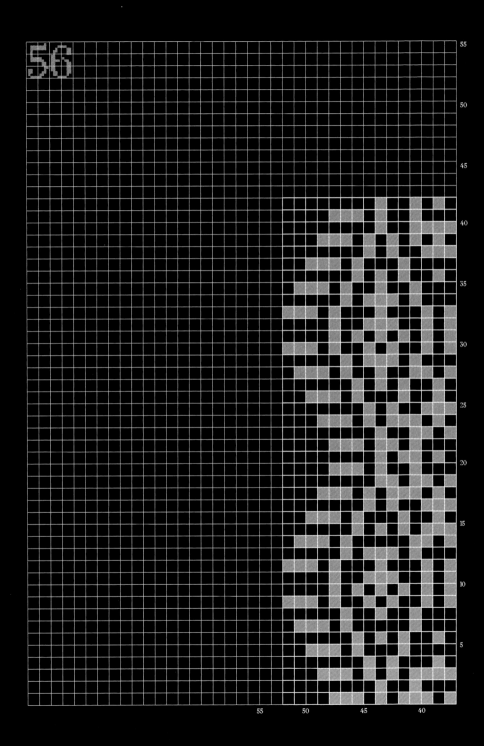

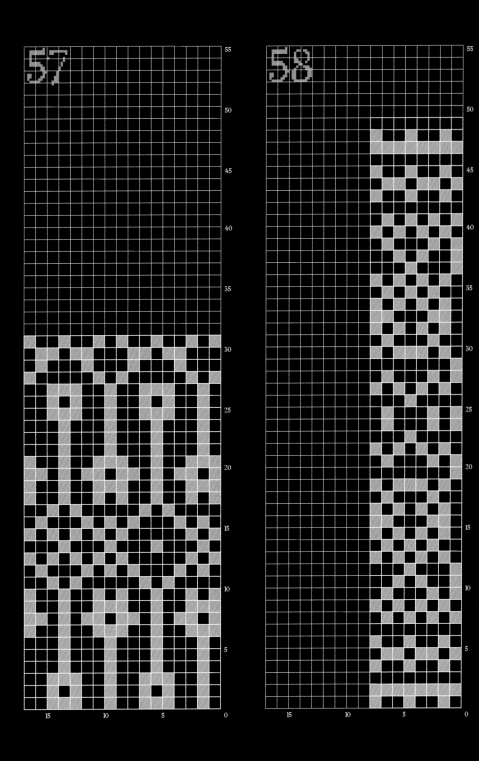

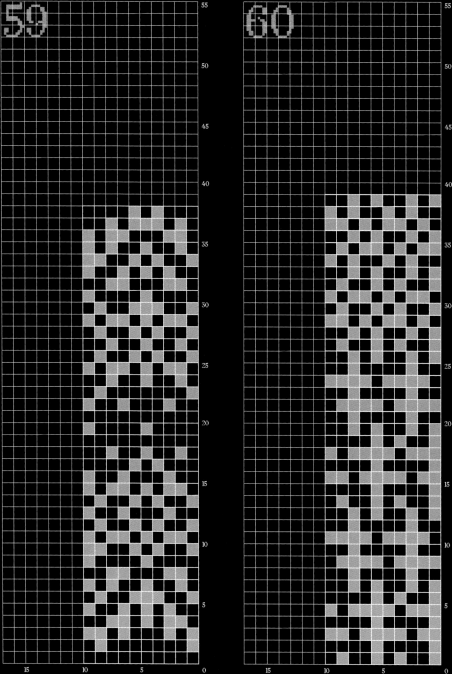

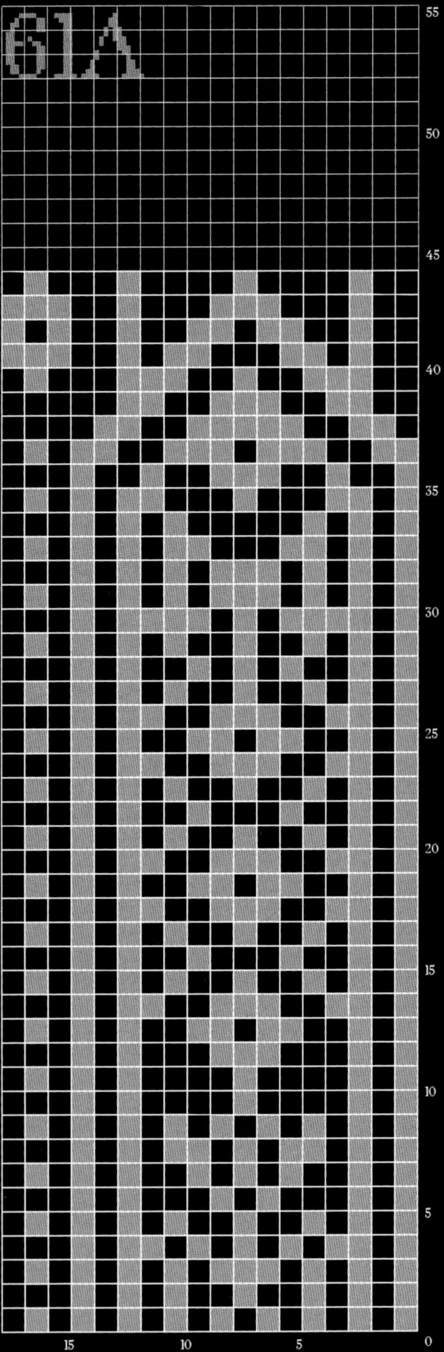
61A
55
50
45
40
35
30
25
20
15
10
5
0
15
10
5

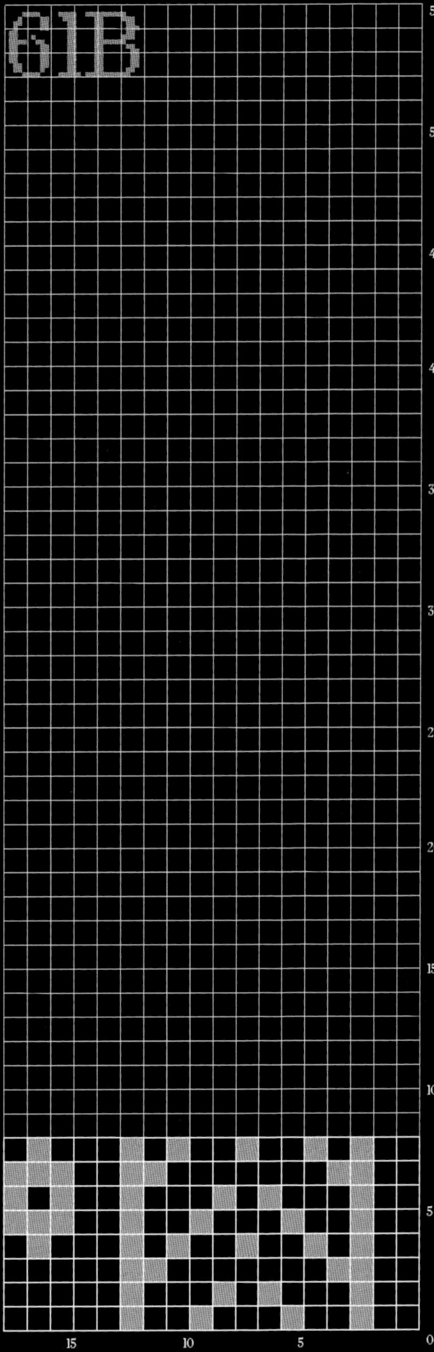
61B
15
10
5

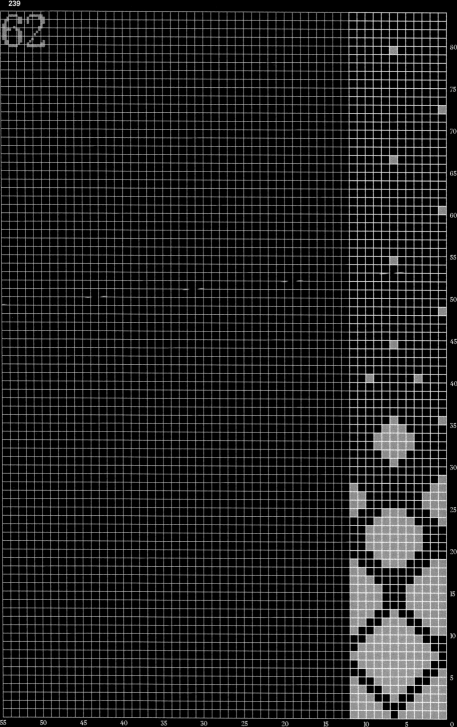

65

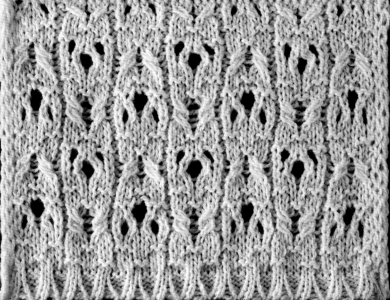

66

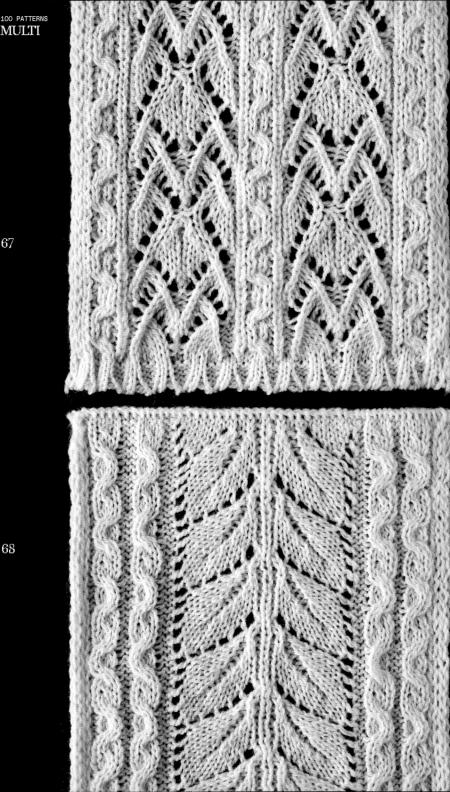

67

68

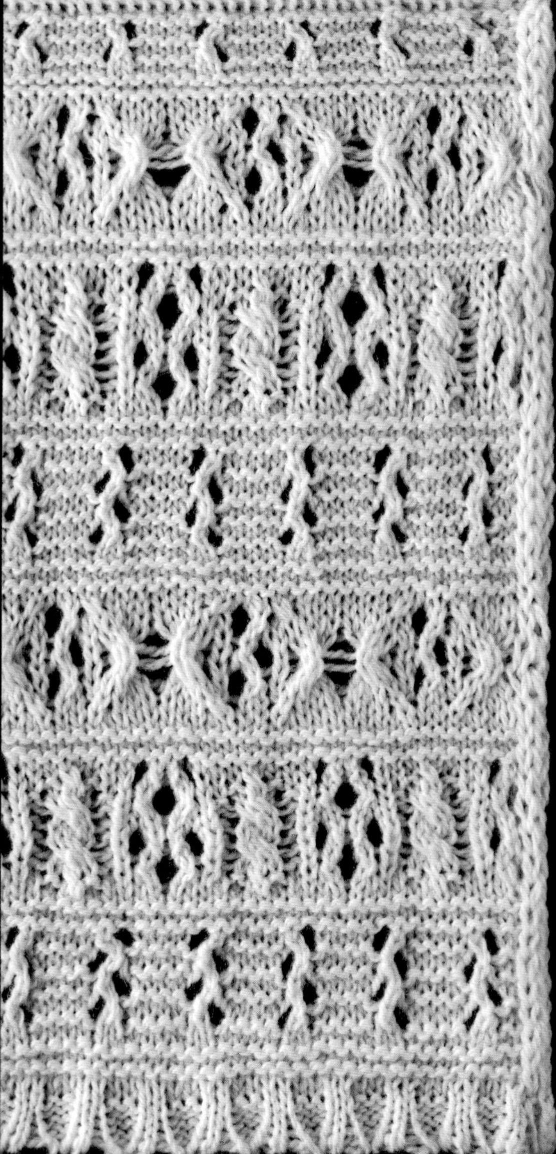

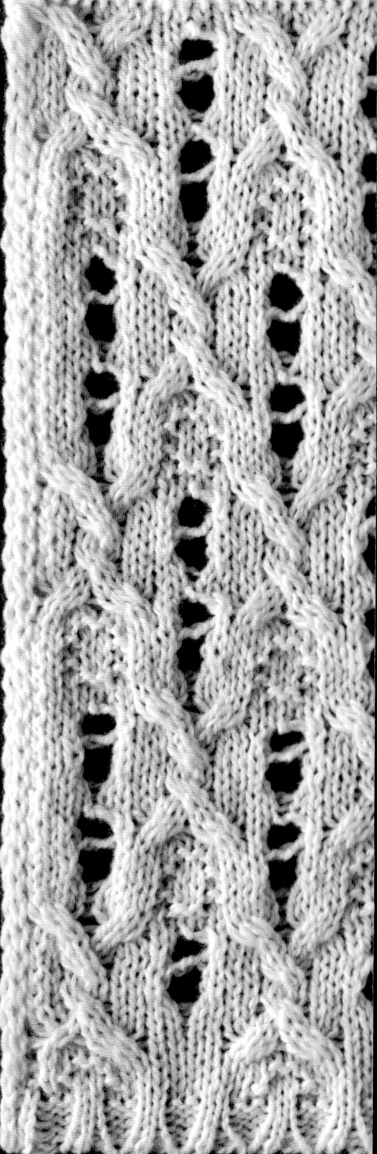

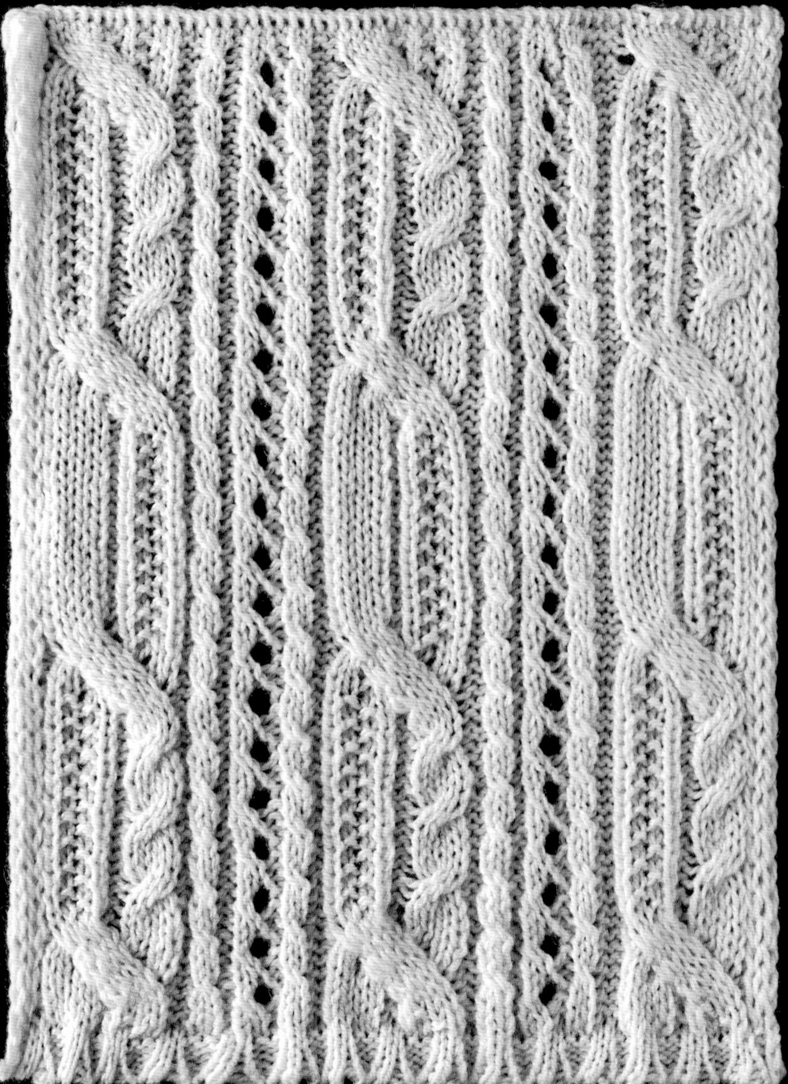

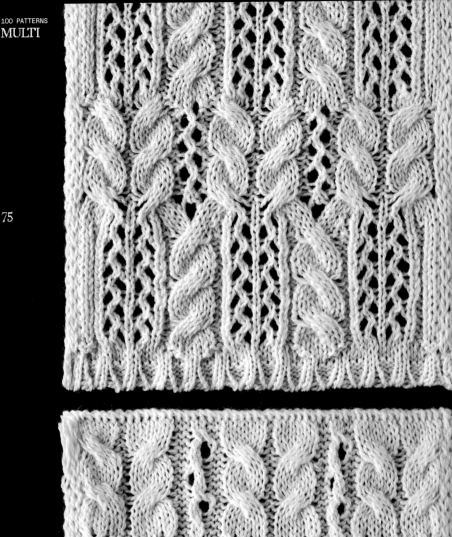

75

76

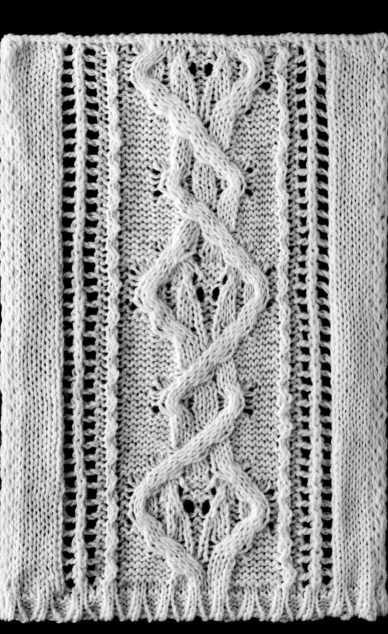

83

84

85

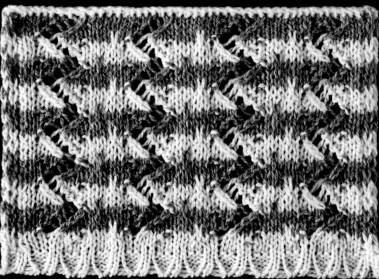

86

87

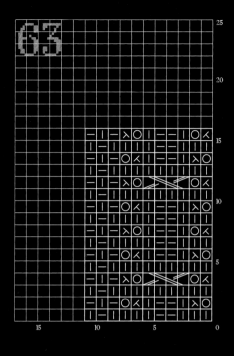

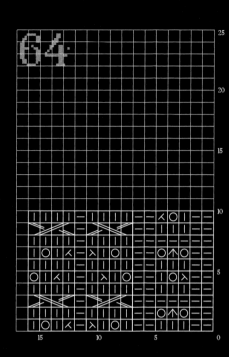

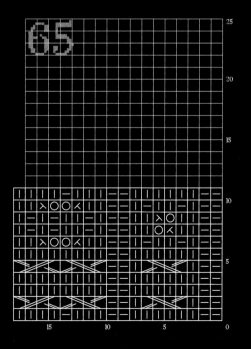

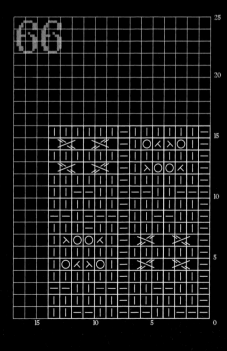

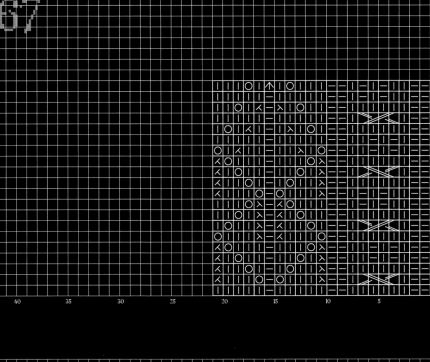

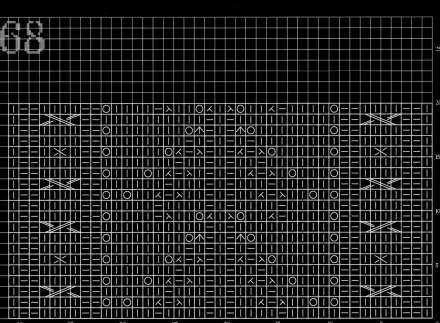

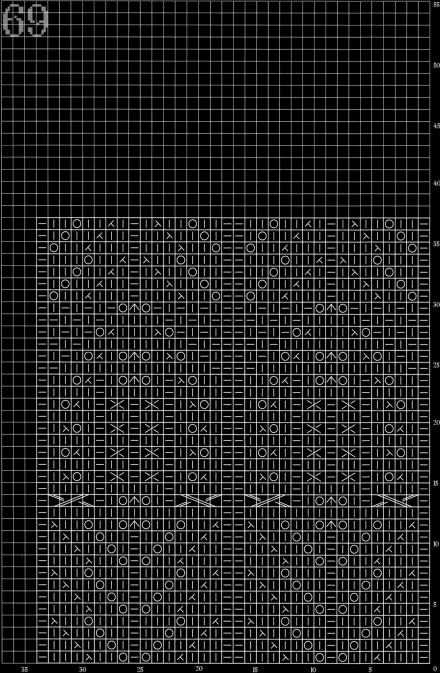

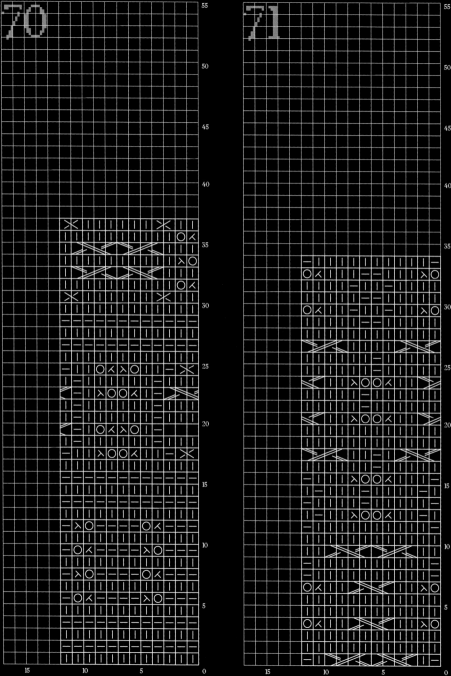

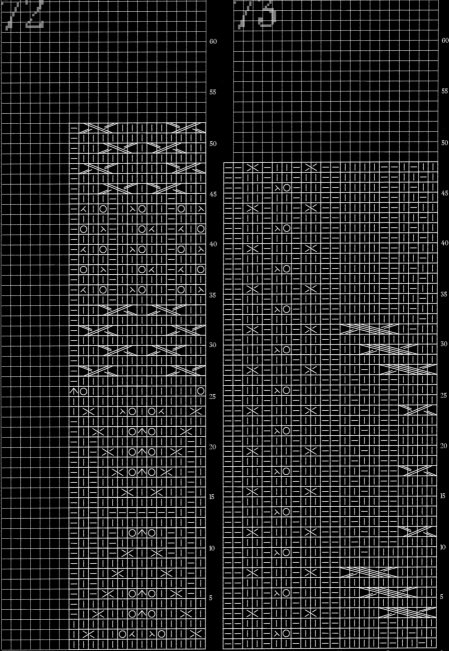

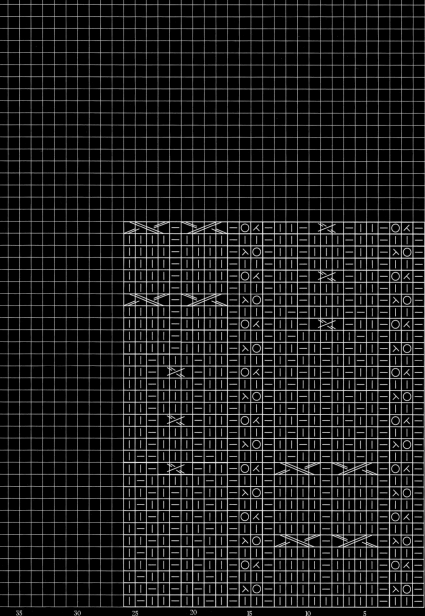

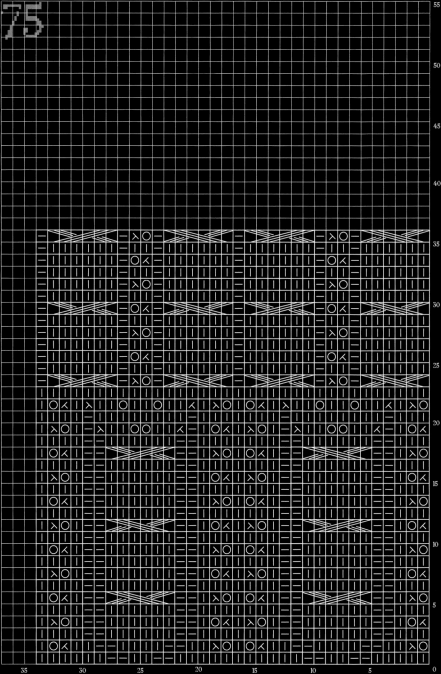

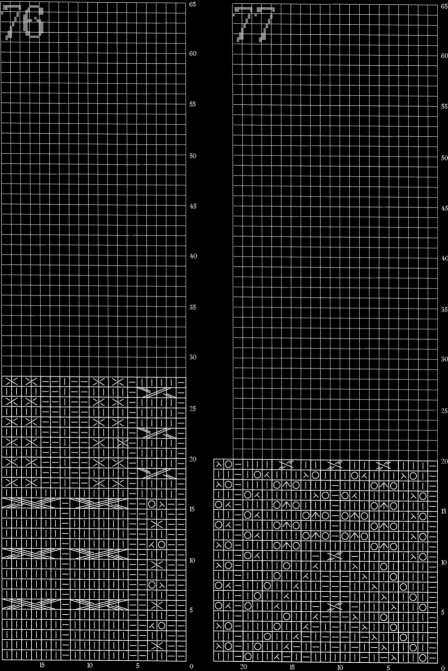

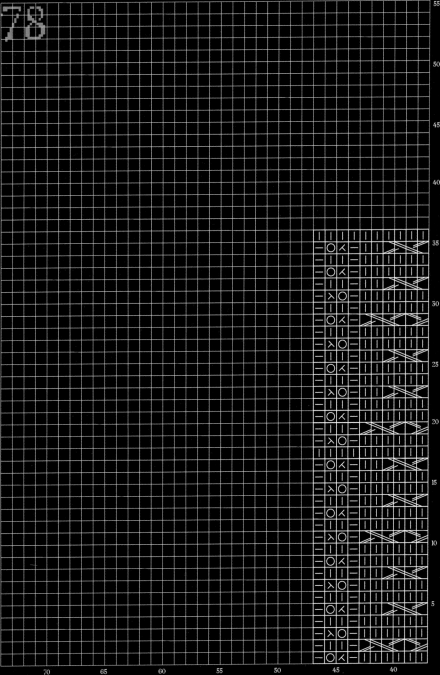

265

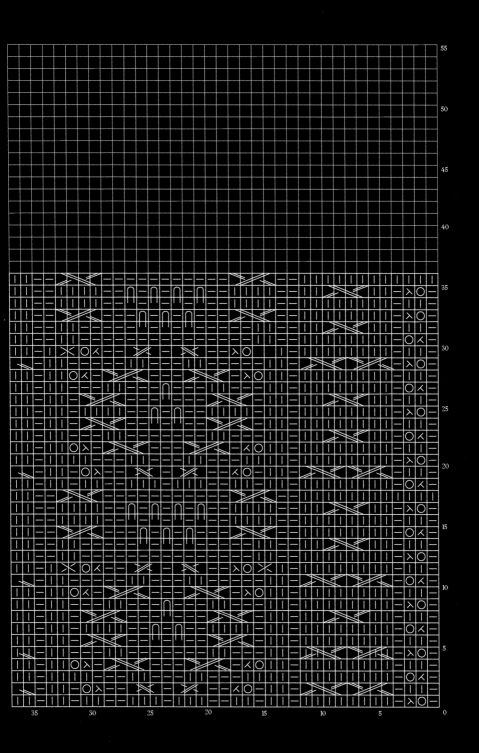

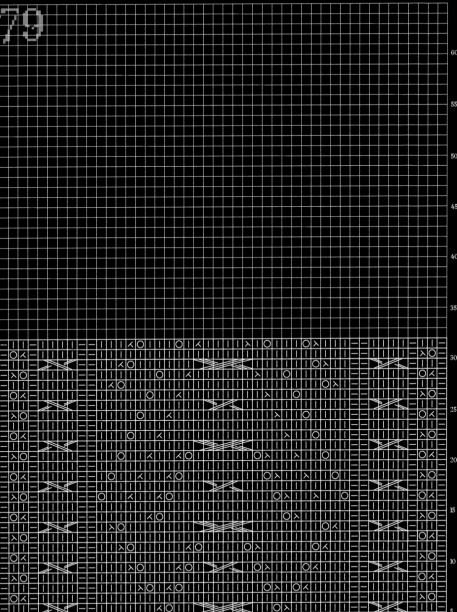

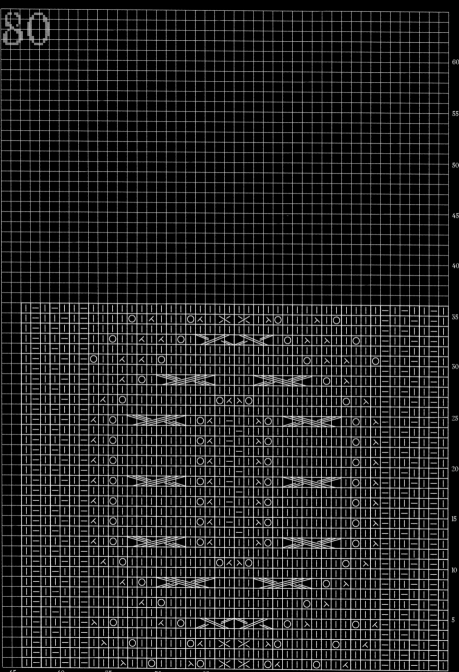

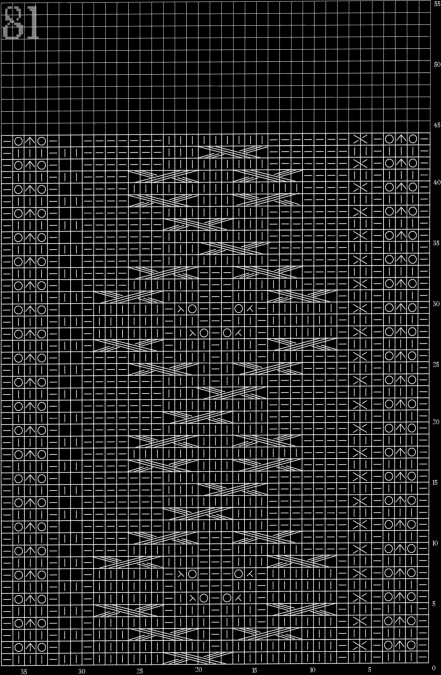

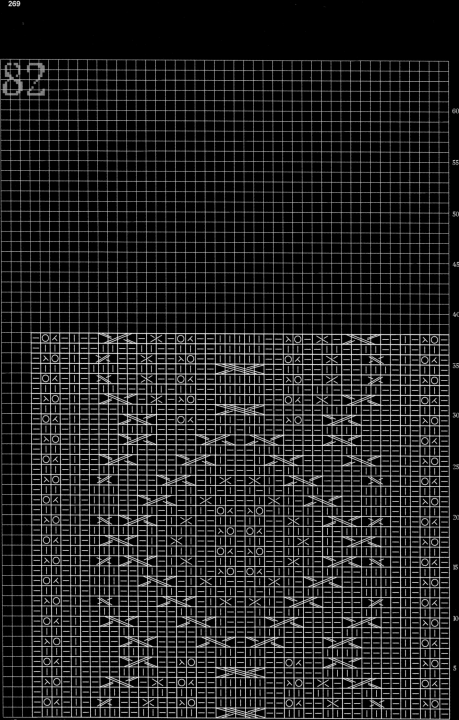

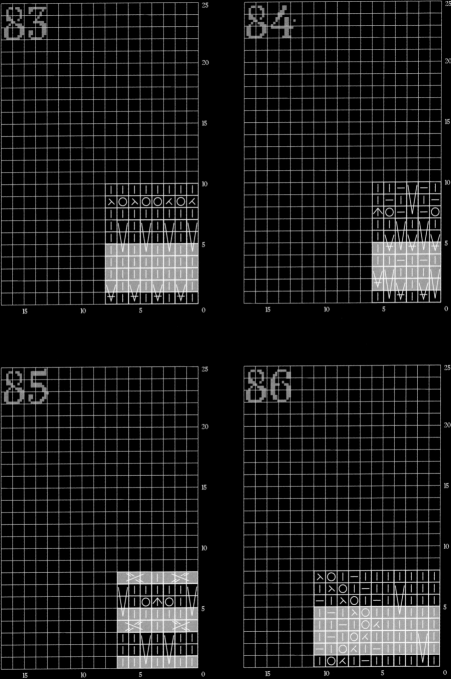

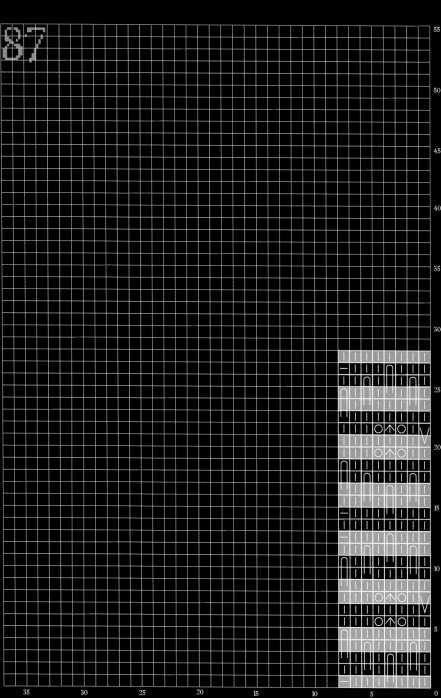

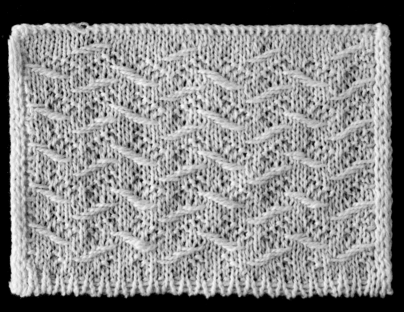

90

91

TECHNICAL
BACK AS
FRONT

93

94

TECHNICAL
BACK AS
FRONT

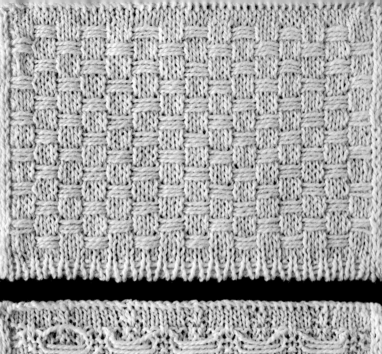

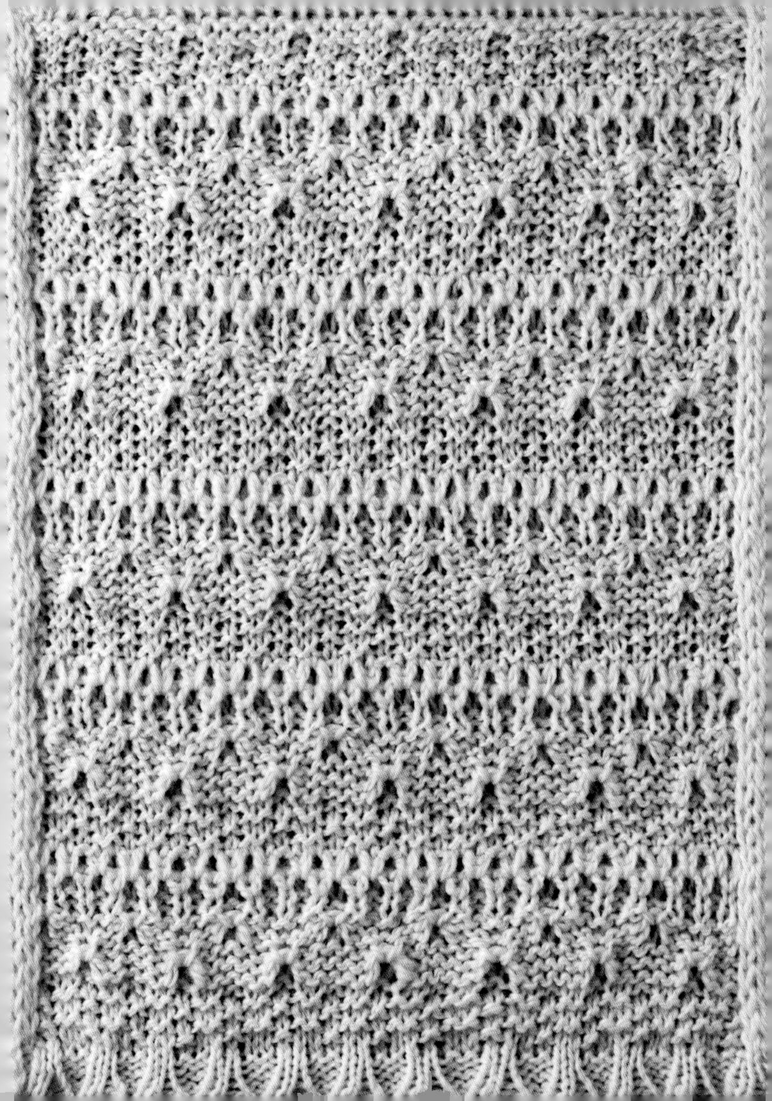

TUCK / SLIP / SLIP WITH FLOAT

98

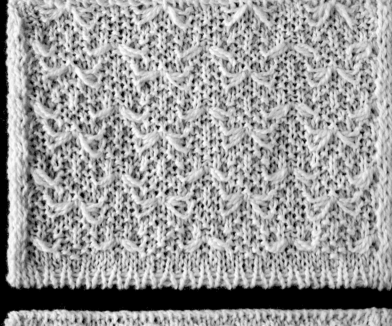

99

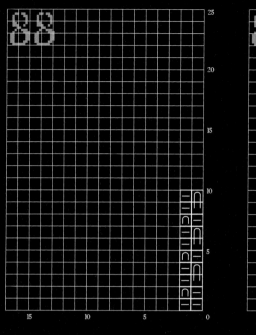

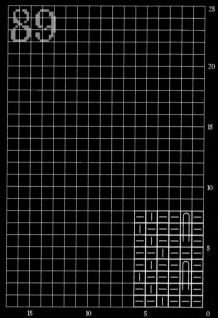

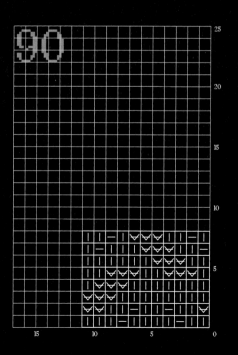

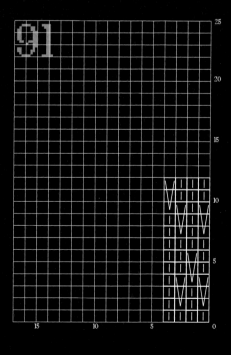

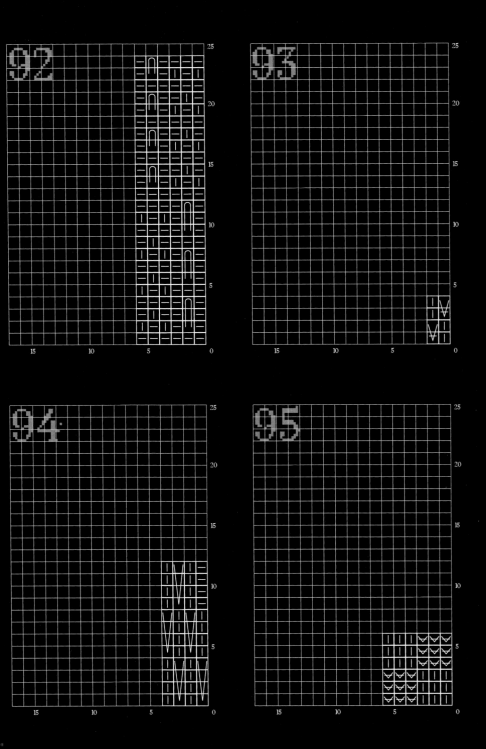

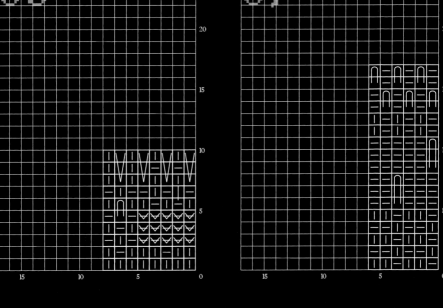

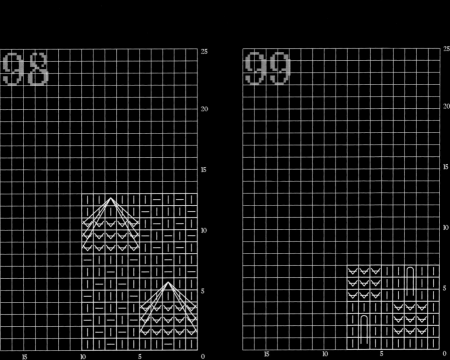

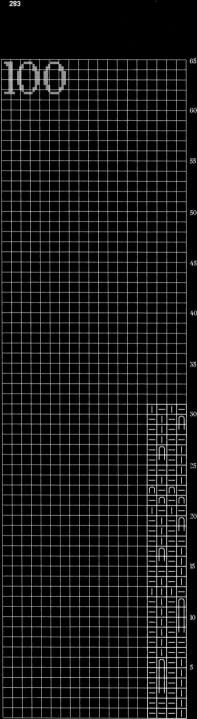

Chairman	PENTER YIP
Editor in Chief	RONNIE TUNG
Editors	PENTER YIP JANE KWAN
Designer	SAUMAN WONG
Illustrators	VIKKI YAU SARA CHOW
Photographers	PENTER YIP JANE KWAN
Copy Editors	BRIDGET BARNETT LISA BURNETT HILLMAN
Consultants	ARKIN NG, CTEXT., FTI, FHKITA CARLA WONG MEEGAN MA
Special thanks	This book owes its foundation to the esteemed "Contemporary Knitwear Handbook" by Arkin Ng, a reference book highly regarded by knitwear experts. Arkin, the former chairman of the Textile Institute Association (Hong Kong) Limited, has been instrumental in the genesis of this publication. We extend our deepest gratitude for his generous mentorship and priceless counsel, and we are grateful for his commitment to imparting his profound expertise to the aspiring knitwear designers and industry specialists of tomorrow.